Banish Sloppiness

How I Fell in Love with Precision While Working in Japan

Paul A. Akers

FastCap Press

Paul Akers: Voxer or WhatsApp (+13609413748)
Emails will be deleted

Written by Paul Akers
First printing, October 2019
Manufactured in the United States of America

Lean comes in ALL flavors

You can read it or get even more insight by watching the videos and reviewing the resources on PaulAkers.net. Or listen to the expanded Audio-Book with extra "off-script" inspiration and added stories of innovation.

**Check out PaulAkers.net for all
his other Lean books!**

THE ONE THING

When I write a book, I want the meaning to be as clear as possible. To make it easier for my readers, I try to include a section that summarizes my thoughts into just one simple concept.

For example, in my first book, *2 Second Lean*, my goal was to teach the reader to "see waste and fix what bugs you." In my second book, *Lean Health*, my goal was to teach the reader how to "treat your body like you would treat a Ferrari." In my third book, *Lean Travel*, my goal was to teach the reader how to "travel light and with a full heart." In my fourth book, *Lean Life*, my goal was to teach you to "know yourself."

In *Banish Sloppiness* my goal is to have you "fall in love with precision".

1) The first step is to recognize just how sloppy you really are.
2) The next step is to be committed to banishing sloppiness from your life.
3) The final step is to fall in love with precision because of the joy and abundance it will bring to your life.

How will you gain this new perspective? We will take a deep dive into what makes the Japanese culture tick and why they have such deep respect for people and resources. We will also look at their obsession with survival and how they developed *big eyes* and *big ears*. Why are they never satisfied and constantly improving everything? I want you to have a *satori* (sudden enlightenment) moment that will unlock a new perspective of this amazing culture. For the Japanese:

PRECISION leads to **QUALITY**

QUALITY leads to **TRUST**

TRUST leads to **SURVIVAL**

For me, the epiphany of "banish sloppiness and falling in love with precision" began one of the most important journeys of my life. I identified my sloppiness and used Japanese thinking to transform my life into a new *kodawari* (uncompromising and relentless pursuit) of precision and quality. My hope and prayer is that this book might also begin a journey in your life that creates greater fulfillment and respect for the abundance and blessings we have all been given.

The One Thing:
Do you want to fall in love with precision?

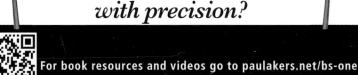

ARIGATO GOZAIMASU

A book doesn't just happen. It's a very deliberate process and I would like to give credit where credit is due:

Apple, for the development of voice and text features. This entire book was dictated using my Apple iPhone and Macbook Air built-in microphone. Then, as I finished each chapter, I would listen to back using the text-to-speech feature. These two features were total game changers and made the writing of this book so much easier.

Greg McKeown, for writing the book *Essentialism*. After reading this book, I wrote down the absolutely essential things I need to do every day in order to feel successful and fulfilled. One of them was to write just a few words of this book. That simple, non-negotiable, low threshold habit, allowed me to complete this book in record time. I never had the burden of cranking out an entire chapter on a weekend or day off. Every day, a little bit and the burden was lifted and eventually the book was completed.

My wife, Leanne, for editing this book. Along with edited each chapter, she provided invaluable insight into how the book could be improved.

My daughter, Andréa, for going through my voluminous photo library, selecting photographs, and organizing them for the final layout in this book.

Mami Takeda is not only a great co-leader on the Japan Study Mission, but she also illuminated for me the way the Japanese people think. Mami san concluded the book was worthy of being translated into Japanese and she tirelessly translated it with great care and percision, so it could be released in Japanese and English simultaneously. What an accomplishment, what a sacrifice!

Jayme Simpson, our incredible graphic designer at FastCap, for putting together four of my five books. She has done a spectacular job, continuing to improve the process and did it all with a smile on her face.

Lori Turley, my assistant, who handles so many things for me, from organizing the Japan Study Missions to managing my social media and slapping me upside the head from time to time. After my book layouts are completed, Lori does the final edits. Lori looks for the smallest things in the hopes that my books will be as perfect as is humanly possible.

Greg Otterholt who has patiently and efficiently recorded all five of my audiobooks. I've enjoyed working with him and I've learned so much. His diligence and hard work in making the audio versions come to life for people around the world are evident in every book.

Lastly, most importantly, all my amazing friends and colleagues in Japan. They have taught me so much about their country over the last two decades. I have developed lasting and meaningful friendships with so many of the Japanese people. Most of them just smile at me and think I'm crazy, but that even makes it more fun. They say, "Paul san, you are so passionate"...as they flash me their big smiles. None of it would've happened without their patience and generosity as they lead me on this journey of discovery and transformation.

ARIGATO GOZAIMASHITA
ありがとうございました
(Thank You)

For book resources and videos go to paulakers.net/bs-thanks

CONTENTS

Scan the QR Code at the end of each chapter and get connected to all the resources.

CHAPTER 1

Nande

Nande is the Japanese word for why. Why did I write this book? First and foremost, I wanted to deepen my own understanding of how the Japanese do life. The idea of coalescing 18 years of learning into one document has great appeal to me. If I can understand why the Japanese do what they do, it will be easier for me to embrace their extraordinary thinking. The more time I spend musing and writing about this subject, the more I can successfully implement these profound ideas into my life. This book is a great long-term project which allows me to keep revisiting the ideas in order to make sure they fully permeate my thinking. Toyota has one banner that hangs in their factories. Perhaps it is the most simple and profound I have ever seen, "Good Thinking, Good Products." The key is in the thinking!

Secondly, as I speak with people and influence them about Lean, the depth of my understanding can directly impact the joy they experience on their Lean journey. If I can clearly and simply show people everything I've learned, the quicker they will marvel at the application of this extraordinary thinking.

I love sharing my story about my Lean journey. Inspiring and influencing people all over the world is pure joy.

Lastly, it is for my pure enjoyment. I love the Japenese way of thinking and it is enjoyable for me to be enveloped by it. I have labored very hard to create a Japanese garden at my home. Every time I walk through and nurture its existence, I feel pleasure and joy. In the very same way, this book is a walk through my Japanese garden of understanding good thinking.

Pay attention to all the details.

So what's in it for you...why should you read this book? If you're interested in learning about one of the most sophisticated and thoughtful cultures in modern history, this book could interest you. If you find yourself in a situation of limited resources, and you want to discover a way forward and prevail in spite of your limitations, this book could provide valuable insight into how the Japanese did exactly that. If you want to learn about a culture that has screwed up in dramatic fashion and then learned from their mistakes, this book could be of interest to you. The Japanese have overcome enormous adversities, both self-imposed and from external conditions, yet developed one of the most remarkable cultures in the world. How did they do this? This book will give you my insights into how they did it and how I applied their thinking in my life and work.

In summary, I wrote this book to:

Coalesce my learning.

Experience the pure enjoyment that comes with enlightenment.

To say thank you to the Japanese culture for all they have taught me.

 The One Thing:
Pure Joy

For book resources and videos go to paulakers.net/bs-01

CHAPTER 2
Don't Be Critical

Don't get me wrong, there's a time to be critical and I'm all about critical thinking. The single most important thing I learned in four years of college was how to think critically. But this book will be completely lost on you if your approach is to point out the problems and shortcomings of the Japanese.

When I first went to Japan in 2000, I remember being on the bus and my *sensei* (teacher), Brad, saying, "Don't be critical." Brad had a good handle on why this was so important because he was raised in Japan and, for all intents and purposes, while he was an Anglo, he spoke and thought like the Japanese. He knew the shortcomings of the culture and it frustrated him on many occasions. But he warned me that if I went around finding all the faults in the things the Japanese did, I would inevitably miss all the smart things they were doing. The goal of the trip was to learn and adapt to smart principles. This book is about all the positive things that the Japanese culture has to offer. Indeed, my life is dramatically

Be a young student, not a critical student.

better because of those principles and concepts and. I shudder to think what my life would look like if I had been blinded by a critical spirit. Brad's advice to me was the most salient a young student of the Japanese culture could ever receive. I have met many people that are critical of Japan and the Japanese culture. They missed all the beautiful aspects and accomplishments of these amazing people. But I have also read many books by those who were mesmerized by the Japanese. Phil Knight, the founder of Nike, described his first trip to Japan as one of the most amazing experiences. Steve Jobs was another one who understood the extraordinary culture and the Japanese way of thinking.

This is my perspective. It is not totally positive, but for the most part, it has been nothing but a beneficial experience of learning and deep understanding. I write this book with deep gratitude, the same gratitude I have for my imperfect parents who did an extraordinary job of teaching and training me and raising me with very limited resources. Were my parents perfect? Not even close. Did they make mistakes? Absolutely. However, I don't replay those

grateful for the people who taught you along the way.

mistakes in my mind over and over again. I learned from

3

Why do they do what they do?

them and I have incredible gratitude my parents made such a valiant effort to raise and nurture my brother and me.

It is best to seek to understand and not to be understood. Don't look at Japan with the filter of the way you do things. Instead, seek intensely to understand why they do things.

On my fourth trip to Japan, Norman Bodek, the leader of the trip, said something that I will never forget. It is a little crude so forgive me, but the point is powerful. After World War II, the Japanese successfully learned from the Americans how to build a powerful manufacturing economy. In large measure, they copied what the Americans were doing and then in typical Japanese fashion, improved everything. Not only did they

improve everything, but they figured out a way to sustain everything, just like they have so effectively sustained their culture and their traditions. Norman's admonishment to us was that we should "suck off the tit" of the Japanese culture. We need to learn from them because they were so astute at learning from us.

On a recent trip to Vietnam, I observed a mama cow walking through a field and her calf was following close behind. The calf was moving from

Norman Bodek,
we need to learn from the Japan

side to side trying to feed. There was a ton of milk to be had, but the little calf had to work hard to get to it. For me, the mama cow is Japan, filled with tons of

Who are you?

nourishment to make our body strong. Sure she's not perfect, but she's got some amazing nutrition to share with us. I am that little calf. I'm moving back-and-forth trying to learn frantically as much as I can. The question is who are you? Are you a humble little calf, toggling back-and-forth, trying to frantically drink in all this wisdom and nourishment?

The One Thing:
Suck off the tit and be a sponge...don't criticize!

CHAPTER 3
My Story

In 2000, my life changed forever when two young men from Japan came to FastCap to help me with manufacturing processes. In my first book, *2 Second Lean*, I went into great detail about what happened. Essentially they told me I was clueless. From there they began to implement the Toyota Production System and to teach me the concepts of Lean Manufacturing. The results were astounding. We took processes from 45 minutes to 5 minutes.

A few short months later they invited me to go on my first Japan Study Mission, so I could see firsthand what Toyota and Lexus were doing. That trip changed my life! Over the course of the next 10 years,

...arning from the Japanese changed my life forever.

I return back to Japan two more times for more learning and a deeper understanding of the Japanese way of thinking. Now let's fast-forward to 2015 and this is where the story really gets interesting.

I'm sitting on a beach in Costa Rica answering my emails. I glance at the subject line and it says "Speaking in Kazakhstan." My first thought is, "Where in the hell is Kazakhstan?" As I continue to read, it appears that I am being asked to come to Kazakhstan to speak about 2 Second Lean. The

BI Group is the largest construction company in Kazakhstan and manages everything from residential housing, road, and bridge construction, to oil refineries. The prospect intrigued me. The next thing you know I'm on a video conference call with Metin, one of the directors, and his assistant, Olga.

Then in just a few months, in the dead of winter, I landed in Kazakhstan to begin a four-year journey of teaching Lean. Three years into the journey, I learned a fascinating story. The BI Group had initially booked Jim Collins, author of *Good to Great*, to speak at their annual executive conference. Jim agreed to do the talk but a conflict arose and he had to cancel. Under pressure and in need of a keynote speaker, Metin started surfing YouTube looking for someone that could speak about operational excellence and Lean manufacturing. He stumbled on some of my videos and he said, "What about this crazy guy?" A few emails back-and-forth and the next thing you know I was sitting in for Jim Collins. When you think about all the twists and turns involved in making this book come to fruition, it is really quite remarkable. Lean thinking has led me on the most exciting and wonderful journey and allowed me to meet some extraordinary people. The BI Group is an amazing organization started by Aidyn Rakhimbayev, a 45-year-old engineer who sees no limits to anything.

Learning to see waste is one of my greatest abilities and the BI Group was in desperate need of

I didn't know what I was getting into with the BI Group, but it was a 4-year journey full of teaching and watching a company grown

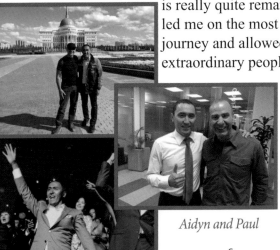

Aidyn and Paul

Lean thinking and learning to see waste. Waste was everywhere and it was difficult to know where to start. For example, I arrived in Astana at 5:00 a.m. and when I was picked up at the airport, the driver appeared not to know what to do with me. For about 45 minutes I sat in a parked car in freezing conditions. The driver finally came back and started driving. We drove and drove and the snow just got deeper and deeper. There was nothing but white snowfields. There were no other cars and I was sure I was going to meet my demise somewhere in the near future. After about two hours we stop to go to the bathroom at what looked to be a closed or abandoned gas station. I took a leak behind the gas station in the snowdrift and got back in the car and we continued on. After a 3-1/2-hour journey, we finally arrived at a beautiful resort on a lake. Of course, everything was white and I was convinced we were in Siberia. The next 10 to 15 minutes went relatively well. I checked in and I went to my room. I had been traveling for well over 36 hours and I was tired and I wanted to go to sleep. I took off my clothes, plugged in my phone

Bathroom break behind this gas station in heart of winter in Kazakhstan.

and laid down on the bed. Suddenly I hear a knock at my door. I jump up half-delirious and stumble to the door in my underwear. I pulled the door open to be greeted by Olga and another woman and they proceeded to give me a big hug and say how happy they were that I made it to Kazakhstan. There I was, the guest speaker from the USA, giving my best possible first impression...you can't make this stuff up! "Oh my gosh!" Olga exclaimed. She told me I was in the wrong location and I needed to be back in Astana, the capital city, where I had landed earlier. Another team of people were waiting for me so I could go on a Gemba walk at their construction sites. I couldn't believe my ears. "What do I do with all my stuff," I asked? She said not to worry about it and to just leave everything in the room. She told me to get what I needed for one night because the driver was out front waiting to take me back. Being a guy who sees waste everywhere, my mind was racing with the mountains of waste I had just experienced, let alone what would take place for the next 3-1/2-hours, not to mention the expensive hotel room that would go empty with the exception of my suitcase and a few pieces of clothes strewn about. "Ok," I said and stumbled half-asleep to the waiting car. Off we went back through "Siberia," stopping at more abandoned gas stations.

When I got to the capital city that afternoon I was taken to the first job site. I could not believe what I saw. Workers in mud up to their calves and trucks driving through mud swamps, as if they were school children trying to see how big of a mess they could make. All while they were trying to build a high-rise condominium development. My head was spinning. We visited several job sites, but at the worst one, they had to drive me to the front door of the job office so I could jump from the car into the office because the water was so high in the parking lot. After

My head was spinning at the sloppiness all around these job sites.

dropping me at a hotel, I finally slept for 48 hours.

The talk where I asked all the BIGro executives why there was so much m and water on their job sites.

The next morning we took the 3-1/2-hour trek back to the resort where I would speak to 100 of the top executives. After giving an eight-hour talk with a few breaks in between, the Lean journey for the BIGroup would begin. During my talk, I

8

asked the executives why all the mud and water on their job sites! I told them I thought they were road-builders and couldn't they build a road that drains correctly so that everyone is not working in the mud? They looked at me stunned that I would be so direct, but then a small smile came over many of their faces because they knew the sins of their ways. Then I explained they didn't have to look too far to see waste. All they needed to do was look at the way they picked me up at the airport. They took me on a needless 7-hour jaunt to "Siberia" and back because of the lack of communication. When I was introduced to speak, one of the leaders said they had invited me to teach them about waste but wondered if they really thought it was necessary to give me the tools to beat them over the head with. Frankly, this was the perfect response from a top leader: humility and not always having all the answers.

The BI Group began to make improvements and even improved my *2 Second Lean* model in short order. Rather than make videos and post them on YouTube, Aidyn decided to break the company up into 100-person group chats on WhatsApp. That way every business unit could post their before/after improvement videos on a chat allowing

Aidyn improved my original model and found a way to make it work for his company.

information to flow fast and easy. I thought this was genius. There is a reason this guy built the biggest construction company in the country!

After my second trip to Kazakhstan, I was asked to arrange a Japan tour to teach the top executives about how the Japanese think. Up to this point, I had never organized or lead a Japan Study Mission. I had only been on six of them myself but considered them to be a life-changing experience of deep learning. In typical BI Group fashion, I was asked to put this study mission together in just four weeks. It seemed impossible, but somehow I pulled it off. Then Aidyn asked me if he should attend. You must remember who Aidyn is. He runs a billion-dollar organization and his time is very precious...he can't afford to waste a second. I advised Aidyn the trip would be one of two things: either a big waste of money or the most important week of his life! Four weeks later, eighteen of the top leaders of the BI Group, including Aidyn, landed in Japan and it would be a week that would change our lives forever.

The journey was just about to begin for the BI Group.

The One Thing:
Do you see waste everywhere?

CHAPTER 4

Japan Study Mission

So after a full 4 weeks of intense planning, the top leaders of the BI Group landed in Japan in August 2016. We traversed the country from Nagoya to Kyushu with the goal being an intense overview of the Toyota Production System (TPS) and their Tier 2 suppliers. I invited Mr. Amezawa, former President and CEO of Toyota Motor Manufacturing, Kentucky and Vice President of Lexus, as well as Tadahiro Kawada, President of Kawada Industries, one of the largest bridge builders in Asia, to be expert speakers. In addition, I asked Venu Srinivasan,

I pulled out all the stops for the BIGroup and it left a deep impression.

Chairman of TVS Group, to fly all the way from India to give a one-hour talk to the executive team about his 30-year Lean journey. I pulled out all the stops and called in every favor to make sure to leave a lasting impression on the BI Group's executive team. Needless to say, it all went better than planned...deep impressions were made.

After three days of traveling and seeing mind-numbing examples of Japanese excellence and precision, Aidyn sat down next to me on the bus and said in his deep Kazakh accent, "Paul, Paul, Paul, I need you to set up training for 150 of my top leadersn. I want to send 17 of them every week to Japan so they can all see what you've shown us." Wow! My head started spinning. Not only was this a great opportunity for me to grow and learn, but this was also a huge responsibility. You can't take this much high-dollar time and not make a significant impact. The risk of failure was significant. Aidyn also wanted me to do it for a fraction of the cost of a traditional trip and to do it all in three days. The pressure just kept building, but in

"FIRST SAY I CAN DO AND TRY BEFORE EVERYTHING"
-Taiichi Ohno

good Japanese fashion, I just said I would do it... even though I didn't know how I would do it. So my life took a dramatic shift in priority and I began to put together the most Lean Japan Study Mission I had done to date.

Every Japan Study Mission, week after week, just kept getting better. I would lead four consecutive tours and then take a break and come back and do it again. Each week we would carefully implement the suggested improvements from the previous week's evaluations. This resulted in the tour becoming more effective, fun, and meaningful. In the past, the Japan Study Missions were all about learning Lean concepts, but they were anything but Lean in the way they were organized. We just didn't eat our own dog food. I was determined to change that. We needed to pull off a miracle...twice the content for half the price.

Backing up a bit, let me provide some history to my Japan travels. In January 2015, I received a call from Norman Bodek. Norman is often referred to as the father of Lean in the United States. In the 1970s and 1980s, Norman recognized what the Japanese were doing and began to translate some of the classic works of Taiichi Ohno and Shigeo Shingo. Norman built a very successful multi-million dollar company based on translating the classics of Japanese thinking and manufacturing and bringing these concepts to US executives. Norman asked me if I would like to go to Japan with him on a study mission. Without a moment's hesitation, I said yes. I was so excited to return back to Japan. I had previously participated in three trips to Japan with Brad Schmidt, my original *sensei* (teacher). All three trips

My good friend, Norman Bodek, translated the concepts the Japanese had developed and brought them to the USA.

had a profound impact on the way I thought and how I conducted my business. The only difference now was instead of being a participant, I was somewhat of a co-leader.

At that time, Norman was in his 80s, and he didn't have quite the following he had when he was younger. He didn't have many people signed up for the trip. But I had established a strong following with the publishing of my first book, *2 Second Lean*. As soon as I put the word out to my friends and followers, the trip was booked with over 30 people in under a week, I definitely was determined to make sure the trip was extraordinary. Over the course of the next several months, Norman and I discussed speakers and venues. I kept pushing for better and better site visits. Norman was as accommodating as he could be, but he definitely was not used to working with someone so pushy and demanding. At the end of the day, I was very pleased with the trip that Norman and I put together.

It was showtime and we all landed in Japan. I'll never forget the first day when we met in a conference room and Norman asked everyone, "What is Japan all about?" Everybody around the room responded, but no one got the right answer...including myself. Norman retorted, "Quality! Japan is all about quality. They live and breathe it." That revelation would set the stage for an impactful week

for all of us. Along with meeting Mr. Amezawa for the first time, there were many other things that got my attention. By the time the trip was over, I made a long detailed list of everything that could be improved. Don't get me wrong, everybody learned a lot! It's just that there were so many things that could've been refined. Norman, bless his heart, was willing to make improvements, but he

The trip with John Shook and the YPO members helped me realize there was mountains of waste that needed to be cleared.

wasn't as eager as I was.

Just a month later I received another invitation to go to Japan with John Shook and the YPO members. This trip was also very good, but very expensive (about $12k). I was determined to figure out why it cost so much and of course, when I took a deep dive, it wasn't hard to figure out there were mountains of waste.

Then a few months later Norman called and said he wanted to do another trip because the first trip was so successful. So this time I had the opportunity to make some significant improvements. Because my name was now officially on the agenda, I became really demanding. Again the trip went off successfully and we made some significant improvements, but it still wasn't good enough.

Finally, on the first BI Group trip, I was in complete control and got to call all the shots. One thing that seemed obvious was we spent too much time on the bus with non-value added activity. If we were lucky, we visited two venues a day. That seemed like a very low threshold when you considered how much money and time was spent getting leaders from all over the world to Japan. I was determined to increase the site visits to a minimum of three a day. I did this by targeting two big wastes. Firstly, travel time. I tried to schedule venues in a *I was targeting two* centrally located area. Secondly, when *big wastes: travel time and getting to* we got to the venue, it was customary *shop floor faster.* for the Japanese leaders to bring us into their conference room for approximately 45 minutes of overview information. I thought we could easily give this information while traveling on the bus, so when we got to the factory, we could go directly to the shop floor, seeing their teams work and the details of how they organized their work. Both these changes improved the quality and reduced the duration of the tours. No doubt we ruffled a few feathers because the Japanese companies were not used to doing business this way. At the end of the day they understood my reasoning and before long everyone was on board with the changes...and they actually liked it. Basically, we went straight to the *gemba* (the real place).

Just like the Single Minute Exchange of Dies (SMED). We did all the prep work on the bus, so when everybody was at the *gemba*, they were getting value-added information and not waiting around for "people hooking up hoses and heating up dies."

Going straight to the gemba.

There were a few other things that I implemented that really made a big difference. I thought why can't the study mission be centered around one city? Surely there were enough Tier 2 suppliers and relevant companies that we could learn from without traveling halfway across the country in the course of a week? By centering the entire Japan Study Mission in Nagoya and Toyota City, we were able to dramatically reduce the travel time and increase the content. In addition, Norman Bodek taught me the concept of turning the bus into

a traveling university. His impromptu talks on the bus were very insightful, but I thought it would be better if we develop a specific curriculum that we would go through over the course of the week. This would guarantee that each attendee would get great information. It was an enormous amount of work--and still is--but I've developed over 30 different talks that I give during the course of a week. It is

like drinking from a fire hose. I've had people tell me they learned so much it was equivalent to getting an MBA. We didn't waste a second.

Even the bathroom stops were designed to teach Japanese excellence. The rest stops in Japan are nothing short of extraordinary, from digital displays of traffic to digital displays of the availability and the amenities of each stall. We used each stop as an opportunity to teach visual controls and respect for people.

By the time I finished the 10th Japan Study Mission I realized that I had developed a platform that was world-class. I thought it would be

The rest stops in Japan are extraordinary. Look at all the details.

crazy to lose all this effort and knowledge, so I put the word out that if you wanted to go to Japan with me, you could do it for only $4,800 in four days.

I currently lead approximately six Japan Study Missions a year. Needless to say, I am never satisfied and never will be because the *kaizen* mind is now in my DNA. Every study mission gets better than the one before. We have developed a very thoughtful survey that allows the participants to evaluate everything from the hotel bed to each talk and tour site. On the last day, before we get off the bus, we send a survey link to the team (using Survey Monkey). In just a few short minutes, the results are processed and sent back to the team so we can "improve on improvements for further improvements." This

allows us to immediately see what worked and what didn't. A few days later we start the next study mission incorporating all the improvements.

"RE-IMPROVE WHAT WAS IMPROVED FOR FURTHER IMPROVEMENT"
-Taiichi Ohno

I tell everybody on the first day this is not a study mission about Lean, it is a Lean study mission. We are going to practice Lean. We are going to be on time. We are going to be respectful. We are going to be thoughtful in the way we leave the bus and every area we use. We are practicing Lean so by the time the week is over, our lives are changed and our minds are transformed.

The One Thing:
Life will present unbelievable opportunities for those who are crazy about continuous improvement.

CHAPTER 5

I Am So Sloppy

My trips to Japan have given me great insight into how the Japanese work and think. I always relished my days off between studies to immerse myself in the Japanese culture and slowly drink it in. One afternoon, in Nagoya, I walked to a convenience store to buy an apple. As a student of Lean, I curiously glanced around the store. It was clean, well-lit, well-labeled, and everything was easy to understand, even when I didn't speak the language. I made a quick pitstop into the bathroom and it was sparkling clean. It had a bidet toilet seat and a sink inside the toilet area. The mirror was clean. There was no paper on the floor and there was no unpleasant odor. It was cleaner than my home.

When it came time to pay, I had to queue up in a specific line that was visually marked out on the floor.

I am so sloppy!

People stood patiently in the correct line and when an open attendant was ready, they waived each customer forward politely. As I stood in line I thought is this a fairytale? I was waived up to the front counter to pay and the cashier rang up the apple and politely pointed to a tray where I could put my credit card. I put my credit card on the small tray and they carefully took it and processed the transaction. They then proceeded to hand me back the credit card and the receipt. A kind

The precision that the Japanese people display is beyond extraordinary .

gesture, a smile on their face, and everything went like clockwork. Totally professional. They were extremely well trained and very polite.

As I walked outside and down the street, a flash of light came over me, I just had a *satori* experience (awakening or deep understanding). I thought to myself, what is it about these people? It is insane what I just experienced. I am so sloppy and they are precise. I'm casual about work and they are serious about work. If I get it wrong here or there, it's no big deal. It only takes a second to do it over. For them a do it over is a sin and completely unacceptable. Their precision and attention to detail is nothing short of breathtaking...from how they manage a public toilet, ring you up at the checkout register, to how they greet you when you walk in the door. It is thoughtfulness and precision from start to finish. They're using their brains. My life is a variable concoction of pseudoprecision, casualness, with a twist of sloppiness for good measure. If I write something on a piece of paper to hand to someone, I pay little attention to the clarity of the writing let alone the spelling.

The Japanese people are always focused on the details and being thoughtful to everyone around them. They are precise from start to finish.

I just figure they'll figure it out or I can just explain it to them. Sloppy, sloppy, sloppy! Not only are my actions sloppy, but they show disrespect to the people I work with. What would it take to spell correctly and write legibly? A different mindset! One that says the little things matter. Not only will doing the little things with precision pave the way for a life that flows, but I will also no longer be impeded and encumbered by my sloppiness. My heightened respect for the small details translates into a deeper respect for others and the resources I have been afforded.

If I'm standing in line waiting to go into a movie, I would think nothing of chatting away on my cell phone while drowning out the conversation of the people around me. Sloppy, sloppy, sloppy! When I flip my shoes off at the door and take no care and consideration for my wife, who has to look at them or trip over them, I am sloppy, sloppy, sloppy! When I produce a video and don't follow a clear process of listening to the audio levels two or three times to make sure they're right, then upload the video to find out there's a problem, having to redo the entire process, I am sloppy, sloppy, sloppy! The list goes on and on. The moment I said, "I'm done!" I determined right then and there to banish sloppiness and fall in love with precision.

My impression of Japan deepened everywhere I went. I walked into a coffee shop and requested an americano with one-inch heavy pouring cream. Within 10 seconds of the order, I had three Japanese ladies stressing out and making sure there was absolutely no way they would make a mistake on my drink. I was astounded again at the care and precision in which they approached everything.

Four months later, my good friend, Nick Kocelj, invited me to come to San Francisco to teach his executive team at Walters and Wolfe. I decided to speak on "Banishing Sloppiness and Falling in Love with Precision." Though I had never given this talk before, I wanted to share everything I learned in Japan.

Before my talk, I stopped by a San Francisco coffee shop to get my americano with one-inch heavy pouring cream. I explained in very precise detail exactly what I wanted...even drawing a line on the cup to make sure there was no misunderstanding. I repeated instructions twice to the cashier. He assured me he understood what I wanted so I stood aside and waited. Four minutes later my drink came up and it was wrong. They used steamed milk, not heavy pouring cream. It took another six minutes and three people to deal with the misunderstanding. As the queue grew longer, I began to look at my watch and my frustration began to build. Can't anybody get it right the first time? In Japan, they were obsessed with getting it right so they didn't have to do it over. It seems that almost every other culture in the world accepts the do-over as part of a good

While on my way to give a talk on Ban: Sloppiness with Nick Kocelj and his tec of executives, I found some sloppiness.

day's work. We are pros at managing chaos. In contrast, the Japanese are pros at executing great processes that naturally banish sloppiness.

So you want to banish sloppiness? It is imperative that you simultaneously fall in love with precision. This new love affair will give you the energy and motivation to slow down and think deeply and get it right.

1) First, you must be disgusted with the sloppiness in your life.
2) Second, you must fall in love, emotionally and intellectually, with precision.

Did you notice that I never said anything about becoming more disciplined? The start of this new way of thinking is founded in deep emotional angst and an irrational exuberance for getting it right the first time! Come join me on this amazing journey of banishing sloppiness and falling in love with precision.

The One Thing:
Are you Sloppy?

CHAPTER 6
Quality

Let's get right to it. What the Japanese have done is distill down the essence of their culture to one word…quality! When you think of the top quality brands in the world, they are more often than not Japanese. When you really stop and think about it, Japan boasts an impressive list of brands. Whether it be Toyota, Lexus, Honda, Mitsubishi, Canon, Nikon, Sony, Panasonic, Kubota, Seiko, or Epson, there is one word that always comes to mind...quality.

Japanese quality.

If you want something done right, with lifetime enjoyment and enduring customer service, and you don't mind paying a little extra, then you might as well turn to a Japanese company because that is exactly what they deliver.

There are only a few absolutes when it comes to human beings.

1) First, we are all imperfect.
2) Second, we all have a keen predilection to be selfish.

The Japanese are human just like the rest of us. They are not perfect and have made plenty of mistakes, but they have done a lot more right than wrong. When you think about the chaos that exists in so many cultures around the world and you see the order and harmony that is consistently on display in Japan, it should take your breath away. I ask myself this one question, "compared to what?" What other culture has the scarcity of resources and resides on an island that is exposed to earthquakes, tsunamis, volcanoes, typhoons, and floods, and gracefully and thoughtfully managed over 127 million people?

Recently I was watching Tucker Carlson, a news commentator broadcasting live from Japan for the G20 Osaka Summit. Tucker was astounded by the Japanese experience, as so many are. He spent a considerable amount of airtime talking about how the culture functioned at such a high level. There were no homeless people, the streets were clean, no graffiti, the trains were on time, and the people were civilized. The society operated at such a high level. I hear you, Tucker. I see the same thing.

During President Donald Trump's first trip to Japan, I will never forget the words that I've never heard any other president say, "...This remarkable culture! You would have to be blind, deaf, and dumb not to recognize that there is something extraordinary going on in Japan."

A few months back I was walking through the Takagi factory in Japan and I encountered a young woman who was of European descent. I stopped her and asked, "Where are you from?" With a distinct European accent, she replied, "Germany." I said to her, in my rudimentary German, "Sehr gut, ich war in den 80ern Student in Deutschland." (I was a student in Germany in the 80s.) I introduced myself and we struck up a conversation. Her name was Julia, and she was the administrative assistant to the president of the company. I said I was a little surprised to see a German working in a Japanese company. As we all know, the Germans are well known for their precision and manufacturing prowess. Why in the world would they come to Japan to work? She retorted,

"The Japanese are so precise that it allows them to see problems sooner."
-Julia

"The Japanese are so precise." A bit perplexed I retorted back, "but so are the Germans!" To which she said, "Yes, yes. I understand, but the Japanese are so precise that it allows them to see problems sooner." It wasn't just that the Japanese love precision. They saw precision as a way to see and eliminate problems sooner. The sooner you find the problems that faster your quality will improve.

Perhaps the irony of all this is as a young child I remember turning over every item that was imported and seeing the words "Made in Japan." This immediately conveyed that it was junk and it would probably not last very long. Today those same words connote the opposite meaning. So much so that the word Japan is a brand in and of itself and that brand screams quality.

"What is Japan all about?"

As I said in an earlier chapter, Norman Bodek pulled us into a conference room on the first day of the Japan Study Mission and asked us the question, "What is Japan all about?" No one could answer the question correctly. Why? Because most people have never really stopped to think what it is that the Japanese have accomplished. They have taken adversity and ordinary problems and turned them into something extraordinary.

The essence of this book is how I identified my life of sloppiness and used Japanese thinking to transform my life into a new level of precision and quality. I've done this through careful observation of this extraordinary culture. This new way of thinking has affected the smallest details of my life: how I shine my shoes, how I brush my teeth, how I shave, how I point, how I manage my money, how I leave a public toilet, or how I give and receive a business card. Before my *satori* (awakening), the way I did these things really didn't matter. Now, by pointing with an open hand, I show respect. By turning the water off while brushing my teeth, I respect resources. By polishing my shoes, I value the way I

You can transform your l[ife] too. Watch and observe

present myself. By shaving carefully. I show I am not in a hurry. If I take off my shoes before I enter a home and I turn them around so they are correctly oriented when I put them back on, I show preparedness.

Norman implanted in my brain that day the essence of what Japan had accomplished. It was a singular focus on quality. Two years later, Julia conveyed that Japan got there by creating a culture that was precise, thereby identifying problems sooner. I marvel at this concept because it is so simple. It's not a complex business initiative. It's not hours locked in the conference room listening to someone drone on and on. It's something that everyone can understand. Recognize you are a slob and banish sloppiness from your life.

Most of us are sloppy: our closets, our workspace, how we clean

up after ourselves, our timeliness, and our willingness to do things multiple times. We are sloppy in the way we greet people, the way we answer the phone, the way we respond to emails, the way we leave the bathroom for the next person, the way we manage our daily to-do lists and allocate our most precious resource... our time! Most people are inattentive to the small details that lead to do-overs and rework. These defects are prevalent and *We are all sloppy.* scattered across our lifetime. They greatly diminish the quality of our life experience...and most of us don't even realize it's happening.

Want to know how to get rid of the sloppiness? Fall in love with precision. This is the *yin* and *yang* of this concept. Understanding you are sloppy is not adequate to solve the problem. You must have the countermeasure and that is to love precision. Fall in love with the idea of *getting it right* and reject the idea of *close enough*. Enjoy the small details. Relish the subtle nuances. There is no absolute in this thinking. You don't just stop everything and get it right and then move on. You pursue getting it right every day, over and over, driving closer and closer to perfection, all the while putting the product out the door and accomplishing your daily targets. It is a continual process of becoming more and more accurate with everything you do *(kaizen)*. It is the aggregation of the small improvements and the drive toward precision that has created Japan's extraordinary culture. Whether making 改善 *Kaizen* a coffee or making a precision machine screw with a Mazak lathe, precision will lead you to a life of quality.

My company has been working with a Japanese company for the past 15 years and they are absolutely crazy about the smallest details. When we fulfilled their first order they rejected the entire shipment. I looked at the product and said, "What's wrong with it?" Everything looked perfect. But the labels were slightly higher or lower by maybe a 16th of an inch. The rest of the world was perfectly happy with our labels. No one could detect it was off unless you measured it. But for the Japanese, that was not good enough. Did it matter? It did not affect the product itself. But it was an indicator of the level of attention we paid to other potential problems arising when the product was being made. We got the message loud and clear and from then on, we applied new standards to not only their orders but all of our orders. Our new ability to see in super high detail allowed our company to move to a new level of quality.

The more precision that is applied to every process, the greater the opportunity for consistency and quality. Fewer mistakes, less time and effort, lower cost, higher quality, and greater trust in the process, product, and person.

In the case of our labels, we told our packaging department to place the label approximately one inch from the top of the clamshell. As we re-defined the process, based on Japanese standards, we added hash marks on the label which indicated the precise spot the label should be placed. Then we created a jig that allowed us to apply the label precisely at the same height and distance every time. We applied *poka-yoke* (mistake proofing) to the process! When the package was displayed in the retail environment, every label was dead on. Before applying Japanese quality standards, we just looked like everybody else...pretty

Creating a standard and Poka-Yoke (mistake proofing) our packaging department.

good. If you're ok with looking like everyone else, then the essence of this book will be lost on you. But if you're interested in moving to the next level, perhaps this is what you have been looking for.

Recently, when one of the most famous brands in the world came to us to make a product for them, our Japanese attention to detail was on display. As the corporate executives toured our facility, they were astounded at what they saw. They sent people to evaluate all of our standards and they could only find one thing to improve. Wow! There is nothing like being put under a microscope by professionals looking to find problems and the only thing they could find was a missed label on a fire extinguisher. Needless to say, we got the deal and we owe it all to our relentless pursuit of banishing sloppiness and falling in love with precision.

Most people don't know this story, but the birth of one of the greatest printing companies in the world happened because of the pursuit of precision. In 1964, the Olympics were held in Tokyo and there was a problem with the timely printing of the results for the different athletic venues. In those days they had large centralized printers and they had to utilize runners to deliver the printed results to each event. It would have been so convenient if there were printers at every venue. The problem was it was not cost-effective to have the large printers at every event. But if small printers were available, this potentially could solve the problem. So the Japanese turned to the watchmaker, Seiko, who was renowned for making the most precise and accurate watches. This company had no experience making printers, but they put their engineers to work and delivered the first micro printer. The name of this new company would be Epson.

Seiko, a watch making company, engineered a small printer that would help speed up printing production for the 1964 Olympics in Tokyo. All in the pursuit of precision.

Precision is not just a vehicle to eliminate problems, it is a rocketship ride to innovation! Not only will innovation thrive, but you will develop a brand that the world is clamoring for...quality, quality, quality! There is no substitute for quality, and as the world economy continues to develop, people naturally will demand higher and higher quality. It makes sense to have quality as your enduring and central target. But sadly most people are seduced by size and profit. Not me! FastCap does tens of millions of dollars of business and could be exponentially larger. We have the money, the resources and the wherewithal to grow to hundreds of millions of dollars of business in short order. I am often asked, "why are you not expanding?" The answer is simple: I'm more interested in an organization that has operational excellence as it's core objective. I relish the fact that I am not interested or seduced by size, profit, or accolade. I want quality from A to Z.

FastCap

I recently spoke with a business associate who had sold over $1.8 million of his product, but was enamored with the idea of taking his company public and growing to hundreds of millions of dollars. After five years of effort, he is now on the verge of bankruptcy and entangled in lawsuits. I hear these kinds of stories over and over. No thank you.

Sloppiness is robbing us of countless opportunities. A determination to banish sloppiness and fall in love with precision can become an innovation windfall just as it was for Epson. I understand that at first  blush, this might not be the most obvious strategy. But for anybody smart enough to recognize that quality is the ultimate target, the odds of creating a sustainable future will be significantly improved.

The One Thing:
Quality is the target.

CHAPTER 7

My Three Favorite Things

One of the first questions I ask people I meet in Japan is, "What is your favorite thing about Japan?" I have asked this question to both Japanese and foreigners. The beautiful thing is, people have given me some profound answers, providing deep insight and understanding. One of the first people I asked was Ron, who worked for Toyota. Ron is a Canadian

Ron explains that the Japanese have been able to combine tradition and innovation.

who has lived in Japan for over 18 years. On one of my Japan Study Mission tours, Ron gave a lecture about Toyota. After his talk, I asked Ron what were his three favorite things about Toyota and his three favorite things about Japan. He retorted that really they were one of the same. I had a sense that Ron was going to give me a great and thoughtful answer so I pulled out my iPhone and I recorded it:

My first favorite thing about living in Japan is the Japanese are so conscientious. Conscientious means not only do you do your best, but you're aware of "what the standards are." Not only the standards in your business and competing businesses, but also around the world. You always keep trying to raise yourself up to that standard.

Number two, we have a real "sense for the customer." We have an expression, omotenashi, meaning a spirit of hospitality. Everything that we do should respect the spirit of hospitality.

Number three, Japan is a wonderfully innovative place even though we are tradition-bound. As I'm living here every day and I'm feeling the traditions and I'm supported by the traditions. At the same time, these people have space somewhere in their heart to innovate.

One of the most famous expressions, when you watch a commercial on TV is, "it's a new product." That's all you ever hear. So how they combine both tradition and innovation is one of the great things about Toyota and Japan.

As I pondered Ron's response, I asked myself what is so different and unique about Japan compared to me? How aware am I of the current standards both in my industry and with competing businesses? Even more revealing is how aware am I of standards of my industry in Europe, Asia and beyond? Tacitly, sure, I make an attempt, but if I was to be honest, I'm not really that informed. Sure, I attend trade shows from time to time, to stay informed. But that's not a substitute for a rigorous pursuit of staying at the forefront of my industry. For many of us, it is easy to get comfortable with our ways.

When the Japanese saw Admiral Perry come ashore in the 1800s, they were astounded at all the modern weapons and engineering advancements that he brought with him. The Japanese naturally felt like they were behind. You need to understand that at that point, Japanese society was closed. They were not interested in foreign influence and they deliberately closed their country and society from the rest of the world. But under the Meiji Restoration, they gradually moved toward an open society. This new way of thinking slowly took root. People gradually became aware of the current standards, both at home and abroad. The important point is they completely changed their thinking. Are we willing to do that?

Another more jarring event was their adoption of *omotenashi* (a spirit of hospitality). The concept of *omotenashi* is an openness to people of different backgrounds and supporting the idea of awareness and consciousness. These two ways of thinking are a deep contrast and change from their original thinking.

It would be easy to just make excuses, "Oh well, we're on an isolated island floating in the middle of the Pacific. How in the world could we ever keep up with the outside world?" Not the Japanese. Their new way of thinking caused them to see the necessity to improve their position. When young Sakichi

Young Sakichi Toyoda, watched his mother struggle with her loom, so he started making improvements, to make it easier for her and eventually invented the first Toyoda loom.

Toyoda, the inventor of the first Toyoda loom, visited an exhibition in Tokyo and saw first hand how behind the Japanese were compared to the rest of the world, he felt bad. When he returned home, he started to make small improvements to his mother's loom. Eventually, after hundreds of improvements and *kaizens*, the loom proved to be better than the Platt Brothers in England, who were the world leaders. Sakichi's looms were so good that he ended up selling the patent to them. Not long after that, the Toyoda Motor Company was born and the name was changed to Toyota because he did not want the company to be about the family. He wanted it to be a great and lasting contribution to society and his country.

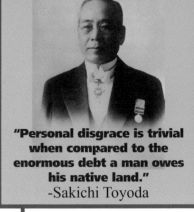

"Personal disgrace is trivial when compared to the enormous debt a man owes his native land."
-Sakichi Toyoda

Sakichi Toyoda wanted the Toyota Motor Company named for his country.

This potential awaits anyone if they become deeply conscientious. Do you feel bad like Sakichi? This is exactly how I felt when I first traveled to Japan and saw the difference in standards between my manufacturing processes and theirs. But most of us are just "fat, dumb, and happy." Life is good. Why should we worry? Why should we improve? Young Sakichi set out to do something great because of a sense of debt and gratitude to his country. A sense of debt and gratitude naturally invokes this kind of thinking and will sustain it for generations.

The Japanese were aware of the competing standards in their business and the standards abroad and they did something about it. The Japanese have not only matched the current standards, but they have now become the standard for the rest of the world. Whether it's automotive, steel, electronics, heavy industry, robotics, or high-speed rail. The idea of being aware is acutely different from their isolationist past. Their change in thinking benefited them and it would behoove us to do the same.

I remember when I landed in Japan 19 years ago and I toured a Toyota plant, I felt exactly as the Japanese must have felt when they saw Admiral Perry come ashore, with his technological wonders. I felt like I was living on another planet, clueless about what real manufacturing was all about. Thank God the Japanese walked into my plant and revealed a new standard to me. At that moment I became conscious that I was operating far below the current standard. The beautiful thing is, 19 years later, my company is now looked upon as the standard. People from around the world tour our facility. Yet, every time I work in Japan, I am astounded at what I see and what I learn.

Another fascinating aspect of Ron's comments is the traditions of the Japanese people did not hinder or block their receptiveness, rather it supported their receptiveness to new ideas. The tradition of having *omotenashi* allowed them to naturally be exposed to and explore new ideas. Ron went on to say that they have space in their hearts to innovate. They are renowned innovators...at the top of their game in so many areas. These are the conditions where "good enough" cannot take root. They are a wealthy country, a highly educated country, one that boasts the highest standard of living in the world. They have everything most of us could dream of and yet they're still not satisfied. They practice *kaizen* (continuous improvement).

When General MacArthur toured Japan after their defeat in WWII, he "likened the nation to a 12-year-old boy." Well, it's possible that he could have said it disparagingly, however, it is childlike curiosity that is so necessary to fight off the calcification that traditions can create. I believe it is the ability to hold opposing ideas—tradition and innovation—in the same hand, that is so powerful. Ken Mogi, a neuroscientist and Japanese scholar who has authored over 100 books said, "The Japanese are masters at holding and balancing two opposing ideas at the same time. For instance, there is harmony and diversity in Japanese culture. There is a great harmony, yet there is

"The Japanese can balance both harmony and diversity."
-Ken Mogi

actually great diversity amongst every individual." At face value, the Japanese culture looks very monolithic to an outsider. Everyone looks and acts the same. But in reality, that's not the case.

For instance, in their religious system of Shintoism, they believe in thousands of different gods and yet there's no rioting or fighting. Everyone seems to get along. Amid all the different belief systems, they maintain a harmonious disposition. Though the belief in a multitude of gods could breed an incongruous society, it is instead, harmonious. The reason is, harmony is the tradition that supports the diversity of beliefs and opinions. It is the ability to maintain a harmonious society while at the same time allowing for innovation and openness to new ideas that is so unique. Harmony in diversity!

Conscientiousness is a very interesting word. It is defined as the personality trait of being careful or diligent. If you give it some thought, it's just the opposite of someone who is sloppy. To be conscious is to be aware of one's surroundings. Notice the word demands a response. There is nothing passive or laissez-faire about being conscious. We should all aspire to this. I try to approach everything I do with Japanese conscientiousness. While day by day it can be difficult to see an appreciable change, when I look at my progress over the years, the improvements are breathtaking. I believe one of the keys is to approach this new conscientiousness with a sense of duty to our country, society, and family with the same spirit as young Sakichi Toyoda.

When Sakichi became aware that Japan was falling behind, this led to continuous innovation, which then led to Sakichi being a leader in the industry. Being conscientious is natural for the Japanese. They don't feel entitled because of past successes, but rather, they feel indebted.

What do you believe? Are you good enough? Are you open to the idea that you are not the best? That is exactly what happened to me when I went to Japan. Openness beget new ideas that lead to new innovations. Is there room for you to be more aware and conscientious? There certainly was for me. When I became more conscientious and aware of what the new standard was, it changed my life forever.

Today I am on a course of excellence that gives back to me like a perfectly placed investment. I have learned to never be satisfied and be constantly improving everything. This new way of thinking has enriched my life in every possible way.

At the start of this book, I stated the reason I wrote it was so I could more deeply understand the way the Japanese do life. These simple nuggets that Ron revealed transformed me and it can transform anyone else willing to listen and apply it to their lives. Good thinking...good life!

The One Thing:
Are you aware enough to be aware you are behind?

CHAPTER 8
Coordination

On my sixth Japan Study Mission, the guest speaker was Dr. Fujimoto from the University of Tokyo. I sat in the front row because that's where all the "A" students sit. It was a very cerebral talk, but he gave us a wonderfully deep dive into understanding the Japanese culture and what makes them tick. Make no mistake, the Japanese know that they are an unusual breed and very special in the hierarchy of the world's societies. One thing that makes them so unique is the way they present themselves. Generally speaking, they make a deliberate effort to be self-effacing. They are very humble. Another thing is they are a highly coordinated society.

Dr. Fujimoto explains coordination in the Japanese culture.

o pushing or shoving, just perfect coordination.

As he presented the information, a video ran through in my mind of all the dysfunction I've seen in so many other countries as I've traveled around the world. When I observed thousands of people in Tokyo Station and no one was pushing or shoving, or rudely cutting in front of another person, I was astounded. Recently, a train left the station 25 seconds early, and the announcer made a public apology because of their sloppiness. Meanwhile, around the world, airplanes, trains, and buses routinely leave late with no one paying much attention. To further illustrate how sloppy we all are, the train apology story has been erroneously reported. Most of the online references indicated it was the high-speed Shinkansen...they even showed pictures. In reality, it was an express train.

When I ride on a Japanese escalator, regardless of how many thousands of people are around, they always stand on the left-hand side so people who are in a hurry can easily pass on the right-hand side. To the outside observer, it almost looks robotic, but to one who understands how the Japanese think, it is coordination at its best. The Japanese realize it is better to cooperate than to compete. I think the idea of competing, in many regards, is a base reaction that humans have. However, the idea of cooperation is a slightly elevated way of living life. Cooperation and coordination require forethought and deep intellectual

Just simply using the escalators in Japan shows great cooperation and coordination.

processing. You may say that competing does as well...and I would agree with you. The difference is coordination takes more finesse than just crushing or dominating your opponent.

When you see coordination in nature, it is amazing. When killer whales work together to bring fish into a circle, they are using coordination and cooperation. All the whales circle simultaneously and create a chamber of bubbles. When the fish are sufficiently corralled by the bubbles, the whales all partake in the feast. The entire Japanese culture is participating in the feast of order and efficiency. Because they work together, they enjoy the benefits of being a coordinated society. The beautiful thing about coordination, in the context of cooperation, is it is scalable...it doesn't matter how big you get, the results are sustainable.

Like a pod of whales, the Japanese have great efficiency allow for outstanding coordination in everything they do.

Check out these three definitions of coordination:

1) *The organization of the different elements of a complex body or activity so as to enable them to work together effectively.*
   One hundred twenty plus million people in Japan can create some serious complexity and organizing them is not easy. Think of all the excuses we make why we can't create a highly coordinated organization? We have different languages, we have different cultures, our companies are too big, and on and on. I would suggest the Japanese would laugh at these excuses. What they manage in Japan, from the bullet train system to sub-suppliers at Toyota Tier 1 and Tier 2 plants, is nothing short of breathtaking.

2) *The ability to use different parts of the body together smoothly and efficiently.*
   This is one of the things that inspired me to embrace the Toyota Production System (TPS). I wanted my company to run smoothly and I saw the coordination that TPS developed as the solution. Indeed, it far exceeded all my expectation, because not only did it create hyper coordination, but it allowed me to build a dynamic culture of thinking people. This is exactly what Japan is all about...a society of thinking people.

3) *Changing from one-foot position to another requires coordination and balance.*
   Make no mistake, what sets apart successful organizations from those that are marginally successful is agility...the ability to change as market conditions change. The Japanese are manufacturing giants because of their ability to change. Take Lexus for example. What business did Toyota, a mid-range quality car, have in challenging Mercedes and BMW? They did it by showing extreme agility. Toyota was able to change and create one of the most powerful luxury brands in the world. I used to be a loyal Mercedes-Benz customer—I've owned three of them—but I got tired of taking them to the shop. I bought a Lexus and I've never looked back.

Of the 100's of examples of Japanese coordination, my favorite is the *kanban* system that was developed by Taiichi Ohno at Toyota. *Kanban* simply means a signal. Think of it as a stop sign, a red, yellow, or green light, or anything that gives you information on what to do next. If you were driving down the road and saw a sign that said "Nagoya Route 55," that would be a *kanban*. What

Kanbans tell you what needs to be done next.

Ohno so masterfully did was take the simplicity a paper card to create the *kanban* system. That paper card is attached to, and travels with all the materials associated with Toyota's products. The *kanban* card coordinates the demand of the customer, the demand of the Toyota production line, and the production of Toyota suppliers.

In contrast, most of us over-produce our inventory and then have excess, which costs a lot of money, time, and resources. The notion of coordinating all these systems and people so that you get just what you need, exactly when you need it, no more and no less, is just too daunting a mental exercise for most of us. Even worse, we deploy a convoluted ERP system that only a

Kanbans can be flexible and fit into every part of the workplace. FastCap has created different types to fit every department.

few people really understand. I know there is some great software out there that can manage these details, but the beauty of what Toyota did is the simplicity and elegance of coordination. For Toyota and the Japanese culture in general, this kind of mental exercise is like stretching every morning and drinking a cup of coffee. They are just part of life and they almost seem to relish it.

Think about what Ohno did. He took all the key elements of the three definitions of coordination and masterfully deployed them with the *kanban* system. He took the incredibly complex manufacturing of 40,000+ parts by thousands of suppliers worldwide and got them to work together smoothly while simultaneously allowing them to adapt precisely to the demands of the customer. All this created a system that is 100% accessible to everyone that works within the Toyota Production System. Nothing is hidden. Everything is visible and understandable.

"WASTE IS HIDDEN. DO NOT HIDE IT. MAKE PROBLEMS VISIBLE"
-Taiichi Ohno

I love the idea of coordination. I love the way it is done in Japan. I want coordination in every aspect of my life and, step-by-step, I'm doing the deep thinking to make it happen.

The One Thing:
How do you like living in Japan? What's not to like? It's easy!

CHAPTER 9

Big Eyes & Big Ears

If you looked at the physical makeup of the average Japanese person you would not say they were born with big eyes and ears. In general, they are small featured people. The average Japanese is a good 40 pounds lighter and smaller than the average person in the United States. Walk into any Japanese clothing store and try to find an XL or XXL size and you will struggle. You can forget about trying to get a size 12 or 13 shoe. It's almost impossible. I once traveled over 160 kilometers from Nagoya to Osaka in order to find a size 13 pair of shoes. I still have those shoes and I cherish them because it was so difficult to find them. As a matter of fact, they became one of my favorite shoes and I wore them out. Typically, I would've just given them away or thrown them out, but because *mottainai* thinking (I will go into great detail on this concept in the last chapter) I had them resoled and restored to new and I still wear them to this day. The

もったいない

Mottainai character

Japanese way of thinking changed me!

It seems like everything in Japan is small: tiny cars, tiny hotel rooms, and tiny portions of food. However, there is one exception. The "large" thing that the Japanese do have is *big eyes* and *big ears*. In Japanese, it is called, *okii me* (big eyes) and *okii mimi* (big ears).

The Japanese may have tiny cars, cloths, food, and houses but they observe everything with Big Eyes and Big Ears.

I have been told the average Japanese person can see in super high detail. One day when I was doing a pre-tour visit to one factory, I had taken off my shoes and put on the slippers so I could walk into the office. As we transitioned from the office back into the elevator to go down to the lobby, the girl who was leading the tour looked at my feet and said, "Paul san, why are you wearing two different color socks?" I looked down, and to my surprise under close examination, one of my socks was a very dark blue and the other was black. Obviously, I had mispaired my socks after I washed them and put them on incorrectly that morning. The important thing here is that when I put them on, I didn't notice. But when she looked at them in an elevator, she could see the difference. I assure you, most people would not have noticed the difference between the two colors because it was so slight, but for most Japanese people they can see in super high detail. It is not because they have special eyes. It is because their culture has trained them to see at an entirely different level of detail.

If you carry on a conversation in Japanese, the words matter big time. The way you address a senior person or a younger person is entirely different, and believe me, if you do it wrong it might provide for a slightly uncomfortable situation. As a general rule, the Japanese can see and hear things that most of us would just pass right over. As I lead my tours in Japan, one of the first things I tell people when they get on the bus is you must have *big eyes* and *big ears*.

There are so many wonderful subtleties to observe and appreciate:

One of my favorites is the vertical parking garage. Most people would never really notice this, but they're everywhere in the big cities. You pull your car up and there's a turntable that positions your car correctly to get it into the parking garage and up an elevator. It is completely automated and your car is parked safely 20 stories up at the push of a button.

Vertical parking garages are just one of many subtleties to observe in Japan.

Clearly marked visuals to stop any kind of struggle.

You pull into a gas station and they have strong visual signals painted on the driveway indicating the kinds of gas at each island. Many times the hoses are suspended overhead so there is no struggling with getting the nozzle around one side of the car or the other.

Digitized toll station to help keep the flow of traffic going. No stop needed!

When you're driving down the freeway and you come to a toll station, you barely have to slow down because everything is digital. You register with a credit card that can be interchanged between your rental car and your personal car. The gate rises in a millisecond as you speed through.

When your plane is departing, the ground crew is waving goodbye and bowing to the plane.

When you visit a park or drive down a street in a residential neighborhood, it is not unusual to see the homeowner or the gardener on their hands and knees picking tiny weeds that are almost undetectable for most of us.

When you walk on a factory floor there is music playing as a signal for breaks, lunches, an impending problem, or to signal the restarting of the assembly line. All the musical cues are different and indicate a different process.

Attention to detail at home and at work.

In most organizations, every morning there is a morning meeting where they do stretching to prepare themselves and reduce injuries. This same stretching routine is almost identical, company to company, from east to west, or north to south.

Elementary students doing the same stretching routine done at local job-sties.

If you go into an elementary school you will find the same stretching routine being performed by children as you do on a job-site that is building a 100 million dollar bridge.

Stretching every morning to start the day.

If you go to the grocery store and you buy sashimi or sushi, it is not uncommon for the cashier to prepare a little bag of ice so your food stays fresh as you travel home.

I would venture to say that if you adopt *big eyes* and *big ears* while visiting Japan, you could find 100+ examples a day and it could go on indefinitely. The subtleties and nuances of this culture are astounding. On the Japan Study Mission, I tell people to enjoy the experience in Japan because they'll see things they will not see in any other culture. It's literally like a 24/7 scavenger hunt.

I once hiked up Mount Fuji, and as I was filling out the permit, the park ranger asks me my blood type. I looked at him and thought, "are you crazy?" I don't know my blood type and nobody's ever asked me that before. If there's an emergency the Japanese want to be totally prepared so they can treat you efficiently and effectively. Wow! They think of everything!

I was riding on a Shinkansen train in-route to Tokyo from Nagoya and I had crossed my legs and the tip of my shoe was touching the back of the seat in front of me. The man across the aisle saw this and motioned to me not to touch the seat. Who would notice something like this? Someone with *big eyes* and *big ears*. The details matter so much more than you could ever imagine in Japan. If you train yourself to see the small things, there's no way you'll miss the big things. If you become sensitive to the words you use, I would venture to say that your life might go a little smoother. When you are speaking, there is no need to use a machine gun of words when a single round, properly aimed, would do the trick. The Japanese people manage complexity with great *sagacity* (wisdom, skill, and conscientiousness).

One time when Ritsuo Shingo (former president of Toyota China and the son of Shigeo Shingo) was on the trip with us, I was giving a talk on Japan, similar to what I am writing now, and he corrected me and said, "Paul san, there's one more thing: you must have *big eyes* and *big ears* and

The details matter so you have to train yourself to see the small things. Have Big Ears and Big Eyes.

a *small mouth.*" Sometimes we spend so much time talking that we completely miss the art of listening and seeing.

I'm sure Taiichi Ohno's famous Ohno circle is founded on the concept of having *big eyes* and *big ears* and a s*mall mouth.* Ohno would draw a three-foot circle near a manufacturing cell and instruct his managers to stand there for hours and just watch and see, but say nothing. The target was to fully understand what was really going on. This activity sharpens your skill of observation and forces you to use all your senses. I could go on and on and tell you hundreds of unusual sightings and things to appreciate in Japan, but I won't! Why? Because I want you to experience the joy of discovering the beautiful nuances of this wonderful culture. If you are fortunate enough to visit Japan use *big eyes* and *big ears* and a *small mouth*…enjoy the ride.

The One Thing:
Okii Me - 大きい目 - *Big Eyes*
Okii Mimi - 大きい耳 - *Big Ears*
Chiisai Kuchi - 小さい口 - *Small Mouth*

CHAPTER 10

The Big Twins

I have spent countless hours musing about the uniqueness of Japanese culture. Why they do the things they do? Why they are so consistent in the things they do? How they sustain the things they do from generation to generation? It is my opinion that there are two principles in play. First, the Japanese culture has a deep respect for people. Secondly, they have a deep respect for resources. I call these two ideas the *big twins*.

Respect for people and resources is like golden threads in a 1000-year-old tapestry. They are woven into this culture and it is impossible not to see their impact. One does not take precedence over the other. They are in perfect balance and harmony and generate power and deep influence.

Respect is always present. When you walk through a department store, the employees bow to you. When you enter a home or a business, you remove your shoes. Respect is present in almost everything that happens in Japan. When the train shows up on time, it's showing respect for the customer. Perhaps you have heard of the "7-Minute Miracle?" The Shinkansen high-speed train pulls into the station and in 7 minutes it is meticulously cleaned. Mr. Yabe, who was the executive that developed and implemented this cleaning system, is often a guest speaker on my Japan Study Missions. He explained that one of the ways he got the workers to do such an extraordinary job cleaning the train was by conveying to them the extreme honor

Respect for people and resources.

of being associated with this Japanese icon. The core philosophy that Mr. Yabe teaches to the 700 people cleaning the Shinkansen is respect. Respect for the customer, respect for Japanese innovation, and respect for preserving the high standards of Japanese punctuality and cleanliness. It is important to understand that Mr. Yabe accomplished this with employees whose jobs are often considered menial. Mr. Yabe understood the importance of bringing dignity and respect to all work. He set out to elevate the status of a cleaning person to that of a celebrity. He accomplished this in spectacular fashion by the following:

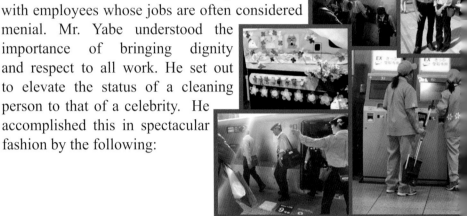

1) He told the workers they were taking care of not just a train, but the Shinkansen, a national icon.

2) He got workers to come up with creative ways to make the job more efficient and enjoyable through daily *kaizen* and team meetings.

3) He allowed workers to abandon the work clothes that cleaning people traditionally wore and to dress up in seasonal costumes. This made cleaning the train like a theater...people (including dignitaries) came from around the world to see the extraordinary performance of the Shinkansen cleaning crew.

4) He got the press to cover the exceptional performance of the workers. Now, it is referred to as the "7-minute miracle" and the team that made it happen is being celebrated in magazines, newspapers, and television newscasts. They even made a musical!

Respect is even on display in the way the Japanese clean the bathroom. When you enter a public restroom, it is normal to find it clean and to leave it clean. To use resources casually would be sloppy. The Japanese use their resources with great conscientiousness and show respect and gratitude. I have come to realize the *twin ideas* can transform our minds if we really come to grips with the simplicity and elegance of these principles.

Bathrooms show how much respect and gratitude the Japanese have for people and resources.

My *ikigai* (reason for being) is to treat the people that serve me with deep respect. Whether it is a waitperson, a cab driver, a flight attendant, or a hotel housekeeper, I strive to treat them with deep respect and honor. I go out of my way to recognize their hard work and make sure they know their efforts are appreciated. I say "please" and "thank you". I tell them they are amazing and give them a smile. I've learned the principle of tipping large and unexpectedly from President Donald Trump. It is not uncommon for me to give a $100 tip. It is always done in the context of showing deep appreciation and respect for their hard work.

I also think seriously about how I use resources. I don't open an extra bar of soap in my hotel room when one bar of soap would do. By doing this I am respecting the person who made the soap, the person who transported the soap, and the person who stocked the soap. I'm also respecting *Think about all the resources you* the resource taken from the earth and the *waste every single day. Are you* impact it will have on the environment to *respecting all the people involved?* throw it out needlessly.

The harmony and unction that can be generated in a person's life are immeasurable. I use the word unction, which is primarily used in a religious context, meaning to have power from God. This is exactly what I'm trying to convey. There is a spiritual element to having a deep respect for people and resources and I believe it connects us back to creation. The *big twin* principles will unleash unprecedented power, understanding, and harmony. When these two concepts are working, they change lives. They impact decisions and infect every neural calculation.

When there is tension among team members and poor communication, it can often be traced to a lack of trust and respect. The Japanese culture is very reliable, therefore there is an abundance of trust. With trust comes respect. Consistency breeds trust and respect emerges.

Are you respected by your fellow workers? It would behoove you to take an honest inventory of your consistency. If we were to drill down even deeper, lack of respect can be the result of lack of education, illumination, and thoughtfulness.

When I see a struggling organization, it can often be traced to a low level of understanding of the principles of deep respect for people and resources.

When I see people get up from the dinner table and leave 30% of the food not eaten on their plate, it can be traced to a lack of respect for people and resources. If we seriously consider the time it takes to plant the crop, nurture the crop, harvest the crop, process the crop, package the crop, and transport the crop, we would never casually throw it in the garbage.

How could anyone throw away all those resources into the garbage?

When you visit a Japanese school, whether it's private or public, there is a prayer of gratitude before the children eat. *Itadakimasu* (I humbly receive) is given for the food and the sacrifice of the plants and animals so they can have nourishment. It conveys gratitude for the farmer and the fisherman that toiled to make the food available. In many restaurants, when you walk up to the buffet line, there is a picture of the farmer who grew the crops you are about to eat. Similar pictures can be seen in the grocery store. When you teach gratitude from an early age, for the simplest things, the golden thread of respect can easily be woven throughout the culture. Further, before every meal, the children identify the nutrition that will be provided to them by the food they eat. It is easy to understand why there is a deep respect for the food that is put before them each day. When there are hundreds of children in the cafeteria and there is almost no wasted food on any child's plate, down to a grain of rice, it can easily be traced back to respect for people and resources.

I have found it even easier to embrace the *two twins* because they have a deep congruence with my own faith. In the Judeo-Christian tradition, there are two very important things that we are instructed to do. First, "love your neighbor as yourself." (Mark 12:31). This commandment is thousands of years old and it very clearly demonstrates the importance of respect. We are also instructed to be good stewards of the gifts that have been given to us. These beliefs are still as true today as when they were first given.

There are some things that are unmovable, but respecting people and resources provides the ability to "part the sea" and make it easier and more enjoyable to navigate life. It reminds me of one of my all-time favorite books, *How to Win Friends and Influence People.* Clearly, Dale Carnegie understood the importance of respecting others.

Let me give you a personal example. I have a neighbor who is difficult. He called me the other day, but I did not answer. He then proceeded to text and call me repeatedly, but I did not answer the phone or his text messages. I chose not to respond because every time he engages me, he berates me. As a result, the relationship deteriorated. Because I didn't respect him, he chose to remove two robotic lawnmowers I was using to manicure 5 acres of his property across the street from my house. Now, my disrespect for him caused the landscaping across the street from my beautiful home to look like a disaster. Needless to say, my wife was not very happy about this. Every morning and every evening when she drove to and from work, she had to look at the growing disaster across the street from our home. A place we had spent significant time and money to looked beautiful, was now going back to weeds. Now my wife was starting to lose respect for me...everything was spiraling out of control. Do you see how respect is such a critical element in how we navigate life? Thank God my wife is better at mending fences. She called our neighbor and was able to get things back to normal and the lawn is now being mowed. My lack of respect created chaos and the giving of respect healed the chaos. It is important to note the enormous amount of wasted time, effort, and ugliness that occurred because of a lack of respect.

When we don't lead with respect, we are only going to punish ourselves with a "dumb tax." I learned about the "dumb tax" in the book *The Road Less Stupid* by Keith J. Cunningham. Indeed, I was punishing myself with a "dumb tax" because of my disrespect for my neighbor. The Japanese culture has clearly not been punished by the "dumb tax" nearly to the extent of other cultures, because of their deep respect for people and resources. They have a lot of people in a small area and still function at a high level.

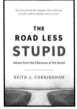

Once, while speaking to the American Chamber of Commerce in Nagoya, I asked the audience how they liked living in Japan. I'll never forget one gentleman's response, "What's not to like? No crime, no graffiti, no homeless people. People are educated, thoughtful, and polite. Everything works. It's a no brainer!" Another time when I was in a factory interviewing a lady who had moved from the Philippines to Japan, I asked how she liked living there? She said, "It's very nice. I have a good job. It's very stable. They are very good at business. My bosses are very respectful and everyone is at the same level. Everybody works as a team. The food is delicious, too." I have heard answers like these over and over from people who have immigrated from Vietnam, Brazil, Philippines, Malaysia, and many other countries. Japan is a country where immigrants feel deep respect.

One thing that is particularly hard to wrap your head around is the fact that presidents and other leaders in many companies wear the same uniform as the workers and work side-by-side with them. This unequivocally conveys respect to the worker and respect for the work that is being done. The leaders are demonstrating that the work on the shop floor is the most important

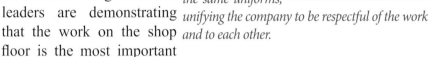

Working together in the same uniforms, unifying the company to be respectful of the work and to each other.

work. They are acting with great *sagacity* in the way they run the business.

Island nation... island thinking!

What is the origin of this *sagacity* (wisdom, skill, and conscientiousness)? While I don't have all the answers, I think I may have a few. When I query different Japanese leaders about why they do what they do, I often hear, "because we are an island nation, we have island thinking!" The Japanese live on a small island. They know they are going to see each other again, so it is common sense to treat each other with respect. You might say they understand that it is in their best interest. You could even say it is self-serving, but to me, it's just plain old common sense. Unfortunately, in many cultures, ego has subverted common sense. A lot of us make our decisions based on emotions instead of critical long-term thinking. For the Japanese, critical thinking is essential to survive on a small island with 127+ million people.

Because they have limited natural resources, they are forced to think differently. In large measure, everything they need has to be imported. If they are not thoughtful about how they use their resources, it can get very expensive. On the other hand, if they are thoughtful with their resources and respect them, it can quite effectively mitigate the cost of both living and doing business. I asked a farmer on the island of Hokkaido why the Japanese are so thoughtful? He reached down and picked up two rocks and held them up and said, "All we have is rocks, we have to use our brains."

Banish sloppiness and fall in love with precision. It behooves all of us to understand the power of this thinking! If you're going through life a bit flummoxed because things are

Use your brain! Be thoughtful about your resources.

not going as smoothly as you wish, you may need to consider how tuned in you are to respect for people and resources. I can hear some of you saying you were raised with those values. I know exactly what you're talking about, and I agree. I was raised with those values, too. But I'm not talking about individuals. I'm talking about an entire society that thinks this way. That is what is so marvelous about Japanese culture. It's one thing for an individual to think this way, but it's another thing for an organization to think this way. It is daunting. To have an entire culture of over 127 million people thinking consistently with the *big twins* is something that all of us should respect.

Also remember, the Japanese sustain a deep respect for people and resources in the presence of abundance. This is now one of the wealthiest countries in the world and still they treat resources and people with deep respect. It is as though they've created a *scarcity* mentality in the presence of a luxuriant life.

The One Thing:
A Deep Respect for People and Resources.

For book resources and videos go to paulakers.net/bs-10

CHAPTER 11

Uniquely Japanese

Friends of ours from Japan, Tadahiro and Susan Kawada, were visiting us at our home in Bellingham. Early in the morning, I received a call from Susan letting me know she was stuck in our bathroom and could not open the door. We've never had this problem before, but I understood intuitively that she was not going to muscle her way through the door. I quickly went to rescue her from the guest house bathroom. I grabbed the doorknob and it opened. We broke out into laughter. As I said there was nothing wrong with the door, I paused and remembered sometimes there was a hard spot when you turn the knob. Over breakfast, while laughing about the situation, Susan conveyed a principle that she had taught her two children. Never force anything. If something doesn't seem right, stop and think about it! That subtle catch in the doorknob was an indication that there was something wrong and provided an opportunity to solve the problem. However, it required someone with acute sensitivity to make it happen.

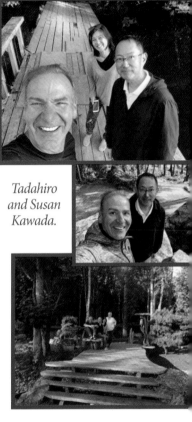

Tadahiro and Susan Kawada.

There are thousands of examples of how the Japanese have solved problems using their highly tuned senses. I have found that most people are not tuned in at this high level, rather they accept these inconveniences as part of life, not as opportunities to improve and do *kaizen*. As a result of the Japanese influence on my thinking, I now ask every houseguest to give me one thing to improve that would make their stay more enjoyable. I have made countless improvements and many of them are very subtle. We recently added non-slip tape to our treehouse staircase to stop guests from slipping when going up and down. I also added a floating wall seat to allow everyone to take off their shoes before entering. I added a hook right outside the shower to hang a robe while showering and an additional hook near the bed to hang a robe when getting in bed. I added a special remote to turn the light on and off while laying in bed. None of these improvements in and of themselves are a big deal, but they make a subtle difference for our guests.

Floating bench for an easy place to take off shoes.

Tadahiro noticed that our sink stopper was not adjusted correctly so when he shaved he couldn't fill the sink up with water and instead had to let the faucet run. This is very Japanese...not wanting to waste anything. So I fixed it and returned it to full working order.

When Susan and Tadahiro toured FastCap, they discovered many small opportunities for improvement...things most visitors would never notice. Susan identified some items were not GPS located, even though the processes were clear and well-documented. She also

GPS'ing allows you to quickly identify tools.

Part of the process was unclear, so we stopped and changed it immediately!

noticed our bathroom cleaning process was a bit backward and needed to be improved. We immediately shot a new instructional training video to correct our errors.

The subtle differences matter and they lead to excellence in everything you do. In Japan, if you enter a department store on a rainy day, there is a clever device as you enter the store that slips a plastic cover over your umbrella. This reduces wet floors that could potentially cause a slipping hazard. To most people this solution was excellent. But for the Japanese, it still needed additional *kaizen*. Like Ron said (in Chapter 7), the Japanese are always finding ways to innovate. They have now come up with a portable rechargeable system that sucks the plastic off the umbrella as you exit the store, so you never need to touch the plastic cover. This makes the process fun and easy and further reduces the chance of the plastic not being thrown in the recycling receptacle. Even though this culture appears to have a subdued nature, when it comes to new products they are swinging from the chandeliers. The name of this new device even has a playful, childlike name, *kasa vini poi poi* (kasa=umbrella; vini=vinyl; poi poi=the sound of tossing trash)!

Kasa Vini Poi Poi.

Sakichi Toyoda changed the name of the company from the family name Toyoda to Toyota. Only one letter difference, but that one subtle difference had profound implications. He didn't want the company to be about the family. He wanted it to be about something bigger. He wanted the company to be about impacting society. When writing the two names in the Japanese

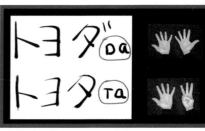

Sakichi always wanted his company to be bigger... to impact society.

katakana, there is a difference of two strokes. The family name has ten strokes. The company name has eight strokes. Ten is the number of completion. Eight is an incomplete number, signifying never being satisfied. So subtle, but so important.

At the Lexus training center, new workers learn a powerful concept: If the worker feels anything different, sees anything different, smells anything different, hears anything different, or tastes anything different, no matter how small or subtle, they are to "stop, call, and wait." They are instructed to be hypersensitive to the tiniest things so they can more precisely find problems. This concept of "stop, call, and wait" is drilled into them over and over again. Why? Because it is counter-intuitive for a new employee, or anyone for that matter, to want to pull the Andon cord and stop an entire operation. But this is exactly what the company wants. They want every employee to stop the entire production line if there is an

Pull the andon cord to slow down and solve the problem.

anomaly, no matter how small.

That is exactly what Susan did when she encountered a subtle stiffness in our bathroom doorknob. I've been a bull in a china shop most of my life, but as I've learned and understood how the Japanese think, I've enjoyed the benefits of finessing, not muscling, my way through life. Are you sensitive to the subtleties in your life?

When I think about subtle, in relationship to Japan, I think of

Big visuals that are easy to identify and clear sides to know when the trash is full.

harmony and flow. They are very sensitive to maintaining harmony and flow. I saw a trash can at a rest stop that had a clear panel and clear trash bags so that the person emptying the trash could be 10 or 20 feet away and see if the trash needed emptying. This simple, clear panel, which I've never seen before, allows for harmony because there was no trash overflowing from the trash can. How many times have you seen overflowing trash cans that desperately need attention? The same clear panel allows for flow for the worker to move freely throughout the service area and perform their job without any unnecessary motion.

If you pay attention when you're walking the streets in Japan, whether in Tokyo or a small town, you'll notice that there are not many trash cans. A while back, a terrorist put an explosive device in a public trash can. After that, the officials decided to eliminated public trash cans, particularly in busy areas. This had an unintended consequence. The fact that it is not easy to find a place to dispose of items caused people to think more carefully about the trash they generate. Bringing a paper cup or anything that might need to be thrown out is not so easy. As a foreigner, this has had a profound impact on me. In any other country, I wouldn't consider what I bring with me because I wouldn't think about where to throw it away. However, in

Japan, I think about it as I walk out the door and it causes me to be more mindful of the trash I generate. There is a subtle reminder to everyone in Japan that generating garbage will be met with a degree of inconvenience.

The same subtleties can be seen at the Lexus training center when you look at all the *karakuri* (automation without power) that they have implemented. It is easy to create automation with motors or electricity, but try creating it using the energy you exert by lifting or stepping on something. This is the very definition of subtle. This requires great skill, finesse, and deep thinking. On the production line, when a worker picks up a metal plate, they have created a magnetic field that properly positions the next plate so the worker does not have to struggle...allowing for flow and harmony. Toyota has also developed a system where if the worker needs 3 screws to perform a particular task, when they pick up the screw gun, magnets dip down into the tray and grab exactly 3 screws. With a simple pass of the hand, the worker has retrieved the exact number of screws without any struggle.

In many public bathrooms, they have bidet toilet seats and they even have a sound button to mask any unwanted sounds from other patrons. Push the button and a beautiful tingling water sound plays instead of someone listening to you grunt and groan.

Perhaps my favorite subtlety that illustrates this concept is the Japanese cloud lift. If you look at the clouds, they are generally very soft and the edges rise and fall. The Japanese have taken this element and incorporated it into their architecture and design. They really like the idea of being in harmony with nature instead of forcing their designs to compete with nature. Like I said before, the Japanese have figured out that it makes more sense to cooperate than compete. If you stop and think about it, nature plays this out beautifully. I remember checking into an *onsen* (warm spring bathhouse) and behind the desk was a floor to ceiling window that allowed the beautiful forest to move right through the lobby and envelop the guests. I have never seen this anywhere else in the world. While

The Japanese incorporate their design with nature... never force their designs on nature

some people would say it was not very subtle, to me it was a classic example of the subtlety that plays out in Japanese thinking. Why block the outside from the inside? Instead join them together in one continuous envelopment.

The Japanese are masterful gardeners, sensitive to the finest details. If you look at a Japanese garden you'll see that the lines are generally flowing and there are no hard, sharp corners. In nature, it's not normal to find hard, sharp corners. Nature has a way of softening the edges. Rivers flow and adapt to the topography. In contrast, when you look at European architecture it's not uncommon to see hard, straight lines, particularly when you look at European landscaping. Of course, there are no absolutes. What I'm trying to illustrate is the way the Japanese think.

When I was in northern Japan, in the Hokkaido area, I was up on a mountain pass and the wind was blowing the clouds over the mountain tops and creating a lifting and falling effect. It was absolutely spectacular. As a pilot, it is not uncommon to see a lenticular cloud that clearly illustrates the lifting and falling that occurs in nature.

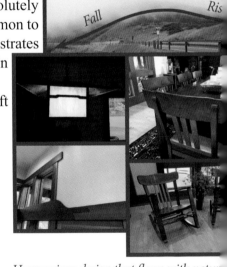

I learned about the cloud lift concept in my 20s while working on craftsman style homes in Pasadena, CA. There were two brothers, Charles and Henry Greene, who were both premier home designers and builders in the early 1900s. The brothers had done a masterful job of incorporating Japanese architecture with the warmth of the English

Harmonious design that flows with natur

bungalow. The result was a home that emphasized craftsmanship and quality over embellishment. They incorporated the cloud lift into every element of their design, both on the exterior of their homes as well as the furniture that they designed and built. As a young man, I became enamored with the cloud lift and began incorporating it into the furniture I built. I also incorporated it into the design of my home.

I love what the Japanese observed...that nature had a natural lifting and falling. It is so subtle, most people may never notice. But these tiny details make the Japanese culture so fascinating.

When you become more sensitive to these kinds of details, it will inevitably affect other things you do. If you walk through a Toyota plant you can see their sensitivity played out on the manufacturing floor. On the assembly line, when a worker needs a screw gun, it is delivered at precisely the right time so they make the smallest motion to use it. They do not even have to move their feet. After the screw gun has swung into the optimum position it swings back out of the way so the worker can move on to another task. All this happens in less than two seconds.

Most of us say, "What's the big deal, just reach one foot further. Why spend all that time developing something that swings the gun at precisely the right moment so the worker has zero struggle?" The Japanese seem to relish the subtleties. It's a dance between the hands of the craftsman, the material, and the end product.

Every time I land in Japan I am on high alert to observe the subtleties that still slay me almost 20 years after my first visit. They are constantly putting a smile on my face as I marvel at the deep thinking, care, and concern that goes into each one of the subtleties I observe.

Think about receiving a command from your father two inches from your face, "I need you to clean your room right now!" Contrast that with your father making a subtle passing comment which sets your mind in motion like, "I heard that Winnie the Pooh loves a clean and tidy room." While the difference between the two techniques is not subtle, the second approach is. Japanese have taken the concepts of subtlety and made it a cornerstone of the way they perform small menial tasks and in the way they execute supreme craftsmanship.

The One Thing:
Winnie the Pooh loves a clean and tidy room!

CHAPTER 12

Rice Culture

My friend, Dr. Ken Snyder, has taught me so much about Japanese culture. In a recent lecture, he articulated the concept of a *rice culture*. Having lived and worked in Japan for many years, he has become a true authority about Japan and the Toyota Production System. Ken explained that because of Japan's limited agricultural land, they had to develop very efficient ways to grow and harvest rice. When you try to feed over 127 million people with available land the size of West Virginia, you have to be very efficient. Over the centuries, they have developed techniques that produce more rice than anywhere else in the world. It goes back to perfecting the process and having a *kaizen* mind. The rice farmers' attention to detail is amazing. There is no room for error. Precision is everything. Further, it is critical that everyone works together as a team. You plant together and you harvest together. Any deviation from coordination and precision could lead to the starvation of your community and your family. If you are unwilling to cooperate with the *kaizen* way of thinking, you will be expelled from the village. This *rice culture* mentality has affected the way corporations think and work together. It is the very essence of how the Japanese people have survived.

When I asked the president of Maultech, Mr. Matsumoto, how he selects new employees, he responded, "people who will not break the harmony." In other words, people who believe what we believe and who value what we value. People who want to be a part of our family and contribute in a harmonious way. What is the point of hiring someone and then having to struggle against them because they don't agree with the way we organize our company? This is *rice culture* thinking. I have often wondered, when Japanese leaders share their insights, if they think, "It doesn't matter what we tell you because you don't have a *rice culture*." Having the answers without the supporting culture is just like pissing in the wind.

Do you have a *rice culture* mentality? I do, and I love it. I love the benefits. I love the thoughtfulness. I love that it completely differentiates my life from others.

On my Japan Study Missions, most participants are in awe of the thoughtfulness of the Japanese culture. The most common conclusion is, "they're Japanese" and this would never fly in their country. But it has less to do with their country of origin and more to do with their thinking. If their assumptions and beliefs were overhauled, they could partake in extraordinary results. Frankly, most of us think it's about DNA. But what it is really about is Long Term Survival Thinking (LTST). The Japanese are thinking long-term so they can ensure survival. We are thinking short term because survival is pretty much assumed. To the Japanese, life is fragile and there are no guarantees. If we are diligent, most of us think about the next five years, but the Japanese think about the next 100 years.

I experienced this long-term thinking when I stayed at the oldest hotel in the world. Nishiyama *Onsen* was founded in 705 AD. It has continuously operated for 1300+ years by 52 generations. That is long term thinking! That is survival thinking! Interestingly, Japan has the highest number of companies per capita that are over 100-years-old.

Oldest hotel in the world.

The difference in their thinking should cause us to pause and ask, what is our real purpose on earth? What are we thinking about? Today, tomorrow, or 52 generations from now? Long-term thinking has deeply affected the way I run my company. For the past 19 years, I have been rebuilding and refurbishing everything about FastCap. I'm not talking about physically rebuilding, although we've done our fair share of that. I'm talking about rebuilding and refurbishing our thinking. When people visit FastCap, they are arrested. They have never seen anything like it unless they've been to Japan. People are working together with a common goal of developing one another so we can better serve

our internal and external customers. There are no slogans on the walls and no posters admonishing people to think differently. Instead, we teach and train our people every day. Our morning meeting is a deep dive into the philosophy of operational excellence and principles of historical greatness. These principles reside within each team member and provide a guiding light to every decision we make.

Teaching and training people at the morning meeting at FastCap.

Another example of how long-term thinking has influenced who I am is what I'm considering regarding my home. I've built a spectacular 10+ acres estate. But, who would want to inherit something like this with its intensive maintenance and upkeep? The estate is meticulously landscaped in Japanese-style and it would take an unusual person to take on this level of responsibility. While I have employed Lean thinking to make the maintenance manageable, it occurred to me that my home would make the perfect Lean Institute, a place where people could come and learn about my work and all the incredible influences of Japanese thinking. It would be a true retreat...a place where deep reflection and learning could take place in the context of beauty and serenity. Again, I'm not thinking about just one generation from now. I'm thinking 10 generations from now. Wouldn't it be fantastic if this philosophical idea about how to live your life could have an enduring impact far away from the island of Japan?

The Japanese people have an uncanny ability to deploy deep thinking to the most important elements of life...the way people work and live together. Without a doubt, their culture has proven to be one of the most advanced and sophisticated, all while delivering the highest standard of living the world has ever seen. Even more astounding is how they accomplished these extraordinary results while so many of their other Asian neighbors have been relatively dormant. Most other Asian countries have fallen woefully short. It is only in the last 20 years that China, rich in both natural and human resources, has developed significantly. The only other countries worth noting are Singapore and Korea. All three of these countries make regular pilgrimages to Japan to study and emulate the Japanese. It is also noteworthy that Japan is a democracy and provides a greater platform for diversity of thinking than Singapore or China. This diversity of thinking could easily have had a deleterious effect on their culture because there was no "strongman" to dictate how it was going to be. But they have managed to sustain their cultural underpinnings despite the rapid globalization of the world's economies over the past 50 years. Put simply, when you go to Japan, you know you're in Japan. The thoughtfulness of this culture has been minimally impacted by the extraordinary connectedness that exists in the world today.

How and why have they been able to do this? In the rest of the chapter, I will give you my take on what sustains this culture. I will walk through some of my most profound experiences and the understanding I have gained along the way.

First, as we have discussed, Japan is all about quality. They achieve high quality because of their attention to detail. Their attention to detail allows them to comfortably work in a very precise environment. It's as if the entire culture has on giant magnifying glasses to see things that the rest of us routinely miss.

When I visited a precast concrete company in Kyushu, Japan, I was astounded by the quality and precision of their work. Remember, this is precast concrete...large structural forms that have no compelling reason to be cosmetically perfect. Nonetheless, they were as cosmetically perfect as anything I've ever seen. I witnessed workers filling pinholes in massive concrete columns and slabs that would be used to support parking lots and retaining walls. Other workers were

sanding and polishing the slabs by hand. Others were chipping away tiny pieces of concrete on rebar connection points, meticulously paying attention to the tiniest details. All these workers were working diligently,

Polishing and cleaning precast concrete slabs. So much trust.

seriously, and with smiles on their faces, deeply proud of the work they were doing. There was not a single person on their cell phone or distracted by anything, including us. Total focus, total dedication, total attention to the details and quality. I never saw one supervisor hovering over them or watching to make sure they perform their work to a particular standard. Instead, they were well trained and performed their work with total dedication. When I asked the president of the company why they were so crazy about precision and quality, he retorted, "because we want the customer to trust us. We are not trying to win their trust for the next job, we want their trust and business five years from now, 10 years from now, 40 years from now, and a hundred years from now." Then I ask why it is so important to have the customers' trust? He said, "because we want to survive". Precision leads to quality, quality leads to trust, trust leads to survival. Herein lies the key to understanding the Japanese way of thinking.

This particular company was the beneficiary of a Lexus study group. Lexus has formed study groups for companies that want to improve their processes by learning the Toyota Production System. Lexus sends representatives to work with companies year after year to develop their processes, reduce defects, and improve quality. These companies have nothing to do with the automotive industry. Lexus does this to be good citizens in their community and to help their society. As a result, Lexus gains the benefit of living in a society and on an island where there are more thoughtful people. The beautiful thing about this is, Lexus also benefits by becoming better communicators, better teachers, and better facilitators of excellence.

This is exactly what we have experienced at my company. While most people are mystified by the millions of dollars FastCap spends to teach and train the world about Lean concepts, *2 Second Lean*, and the Toyota Production System, we understand that we are really the true beneficiaries. Our people are deeply proud of the work they do and are gratified that they're able to help other people from around the world. We have become better communicators, teachers, team members, and thought leaders. In addition, I personally am so much more satisfied that my work has helped so many people. It is not the size of my bank account that brings me joy. It is the size of the network of thoughtful people around the world that I know and call my friends.

This is what I love about Japan, and particularly Lexus and Toyota. This is a page from the book Steve Jobs: Thinking Differently by Patricia Lakin. Toyota and Lexus think differently. FastCap thinks differently. We do the opposite of what common business practices suggest. We are not thinking about ourselves or the bottom-line. We have fully embraced a different way of thinking.

This is what I love about Japan, and particularly Lexus and Toyota. This is what Steve Jobs always did...think different! FastCap thinks different. We do the opposite of what common business practices suggest. We are not thinking about ourselves or the bottom-line. We have fully embraced a different way of thinking.

Japan is an island floating in the Pacific, battered by harsh geological and climatic conditions. It is a struggle to survive. But to the Japanese, it's life. It's a challenge and it requires a *kaizen* mind. The vast majority of the island is mountainous and not inhabitable. As a result, the majority of the population lives in the coastal areas. Flatland is very scarce and at a premium, so they cannot afford to waste a single square inch. It is an island approximately the size of California with three times as many people. Can you even imagine what California would look like with 127+ million people...three times the current population.

Survival has been at the forefront of their thinking for a long time. Even though they have achieved great luxury and economic success, they have not allowed this luxury to make them lazy or complacent. Instead, they have fully embraced a survival mentality, because, regardless of their success, a catastrophe could be right around the corner. In most cultures, as more accouterments and luxury are acquired, there is a tendency for it to breed passivity and laziness. The Japanese have not succumbed to this. The more successful they become, the harder they work, and the more thoughtfulness they exhibit.

There are many reasons they've been able to eschew this natural condition. First is the concept of survival. They have learned from past mistakes. For instance, the Japanese leadership went headlong into World War II not thinking rationally about attacking the largest country in the world (China), and the most powerful country in the world (the United States). Instead, they acted irrationally and nearly evaporated their entire country. They learned valuable lessons and did a deep *hansei* (acknowledge mistakes) and replaced the irrational with the rational. They walked right to the edge of a cliff and stared down into the pit, and collectively as a society said, "never again." Survival is paramount and they conduct themselves with this rational long-term thinking.

When I was in a Tier 1 Lexus supplier, I was watching them measure a sixth of a second out of a process. I asked the president if it stressed him out to have to pay attention to this level of detail? He told me, "as Japanese we don't know the word stress. If we don't do this, we don't survive. China is one day away from us. It is weeks away from you (the United States). There is an entirely different level of urgency for us."

Attention to detail.

The second reason is they are naturally self-effacing. In their minds, they are never good enough. As a culture, they've been able to maintain this disposition and it serves them well. It has allowed them to be consistently curious and never really satisfied. A few years ago, I organized a US tour for Ritsuo Shingo (son of Shigeo Shingo). I put together about 10 companies that I felt would benefit from having Ritsuo spend a few days evaluating their processes. Afterward, I ask him about the tour. As he began to speak, I knew he would enumerate profound wisdom, so I pulled out my iPhone and began to record. I asked him about the company that he was most impressed with and the company that he was least impressed with and it all came down to one stray nail. He explained that one of the companies he visited had shot a nail through a piece of wood and it came out the other side. He asked them why there was a defect and they replied it didn't matter, no one would see it. Ritsuo said that is not correct, quality is seen and unseen. Quality should extend through the entire project. He then went on to ask why did the nail come out of the wood? Because there was a knot in the wood. Why was there a knot in the wood? Because they didn't see the knot before they installed the wood trim. Why do you order material that has knots in it? Because the supplier gave them wood with knots. Ritsuo said you must go upstream, go to the source of the problem. That is where quality starts and precision can flourish. We continued to discuss why this is so important and to my astonishment, Ritsuo lead me sequentially through the deep

understanding that I had come to love and appreciate about Japan. Quality leads to trust, trust leads to survival.

I am acutely aware that there is no certainty that all the work and effort I have expended in my life will endure in my lifetime, let alone generations to come.

Ritsuo Shingo

However, I have come to realize with certainty, that an individual, organization, or society that focuses on quality has a much higher probability of survival. The specific path to achieve survival is to love precision, which eliminates defects. Fewer defects, and higher quality lead to customers that return generation after generation. The quality experience, not the slick marketing and sales program is what keeps drawing back customers. This creates trust because of the dependable and predictable nature of the relationship.

There are so many enigmas about Japan, but perhaps the greatest of all is that in their obsession with survival, they have created a platform by which they are able to live at a level far beyond simply feeding themselves. Think of the creativity that can flourish in an environment when you're not obsessed with surviving, but you're obsessed with the details about how you will survive. The details of the processes have created abundance. Not only have you created a model that makes sustainability more likely, by default, you created a process that demands creativity and in doing so, you become more creative and prosperous. So what's more important, survival or the details of how you will survive? Therein lies my thesis, "banish sloppiness and fall in love with precision!"

The One Thing:
Sloppiness is a sure guarantee that survival is no guarantee!

CHAPTER 13
My Favorite Word

I could regale you with hundreds of stories that elucidate the uniqueness of the Japanese culture. Each of my experiences has slowly and methodically shaped my opinion of what Japan is all about. I believe you would find all these experiences interesting and supportive of my thesis. However, the purpose of this book is not to tell you everything but to whet your appetite and stimulate your curiosity in hopes you might find some benefit to deploy elements of Japanese thinking into your own life. If you should be fortunate enough to travel to Japan and study and learn about this culture, I think your life would be enhanced.

Enhance your life by studying and learning this culture.

As of the writing of this book, I have trained over 500 people from around the world in Japan. I have crisscrossed Japan in trains, planes, automobiles, and even motorcycles. I have met and worked with some of the top leaders and thinkers. I have lead groups through factories, businesses, and construction sites to demonstrate, illustrate, and contrast what makes the Japanese culture so unique. I have seen people literally in tears and speechless after walking out of Toyota and Lexus facilities, shaking their heads in disbelief, stating that what they saw was impossible. But of all the places and spectacular manufacturing facilities that I've shown to people, nothing has made a bigger or lasting impact than visiting a Japanese elementary school. This is where we pull back the curtain to understand this amazing

69

culture. It is the children of Japan that grow up to be the leaders that sustain this culture. At school, they are not managing the tardiness or misbehavior of the students. They are not cajoling, prodding, or pleading with the children to behave and learn. They are not disciplining kids because of bullying or an unhealthy obsession with their cell phones. They have a zero bullying policy and cell phones are not allowed. Instead, you see thoughtful, calm, rational adults that are treating children as adults. Every day the children come together to learn, grow, and improve. There is a *kata* (routine) that happens every day in Japanese schools. There are no janitors, with the exception of those doing specialized work such as cleaning windows in multi-story buildings. Otherwise, the children clean the schools from the toilets, the sinks, the cafeteria, the hallways, the windows, the coat rooms, the playground, to the gardens. In most countries, this would be considered child abuse. In Japan, this kind of work wells up from the philosophy within this culture, showing deep respect for people and things. When it's lunchtime, the magic begins. Hundreds of students come into a cafeteria. They are well behaved and sit respectfully as team leaders from every table serve them their lunch. As the food is distributed, not one child eats a single morsel until everyone is served and the prayer of gratefulness is given.

Then a student explains what the food is that they're about to eat and nutrition they will gain from the food. There are no sugary drinks or sugary desserts, there is just healthy vegetables, rice, and fish to eat and milk to drink. Each child eats the food that is given and if there is a chance they will not be able to eat all the food, before they ever touch their plate, they stand up and go over to the food serving area and explain what food they would like removed respectfully from their plate so it is not wasted. Then they proceed back to their table where they eat all the food on their plate. At the end of the meal, everyone works together to clean up the entire cafeteria. What is so remarkable is that there is almost no wasted food. There is no large trash can where they dispose food that has gone uneaten. That would be *mottainai*!

Mottainai character

I would like to end this book by discussing my favorite Japanese word, the word that has made the most profound impact on my thinking: *mottainai*. It simply means to have a deep sense of regret when you waste anything. If they leave a grain of rice on the plate, that is *mottainai*. If they leave the water running when they brush their teeth, that is *mottainai*. When children demonstrate a supreme stewardship over the resources that they have been given, even down to a wasted grain of rice, it is extraordinary! Since I have learned this word, *mottainai*, and have seen the deep meaning of it played out in schools across this country, my thinking has forever changed. In everything I do the word *mottainai* rings in my ears. What a pity to waste! Why would I throw in the trash the effort the farmer has spent to provide food. Why would I waste the precious resources of my country? Why would I be so careless with the time and thoughtfulness of another human being on my behalf? This is the *mottainai* thinking and this thinking has changed me forever.

One time I interviewed a nun who was the head administrator at a Christian school in Japan. The fact that there are Christian schools in a culture that is largely Shinto and Buddhist, should give everyone pause. How could this be? Every day the children learn about

Christianity, say the Lord's Prayer, and yet they are not Christian. This is a giant enigma, so difficult to understand, but so Japanese. They are learning about other cultures, languages, and religions and they do it all with smiles on their faces. They're not threatened by the idea of Christianity spreading rapidly across their country. Rather they are elevating themselves in their thinking and understanding as they learn about other cultures. The Christians who are managing these schools are not forcing their religious practices on the children, rather they are respectfully teaching and training them. In any other culture, you would expect tension or an insular attitude toward other cultures and beliefs, but in Japan, it is not the case. As we were walking down the hallways and watching the children happily clean the entire school, I stopped to greet the head nun and ask a few questions. Why did she like Japan? She explained she had lived there for 40 years and was originally from Canada. She told me that Japan is so safe, so peaceful, and a beautiful country. She said, "I like the people very much and they're good people, very good people." When she travels home to Canada periodically and returns back to Japan she always tells people, "I am back".

There is something very special about this country! It all comes down to a single grain of rice. Why would you throw a single grain of rice in the trash? That single grain represents the effort of a single individual who planted the seed, nurtured the seed, irrigated the seed, harvested the seed, and transported rice to villages, schools, and cities across the country. Wrapped up in that single grain of rice is the word *mottainai*. What a pity to waste anything. It is with this single idea that this culture and country has differentiated itself from the rest of the world. It is with this single idea that my life and my company were transformed. Toyota understood that they could not be wasteful and survive. They had to find a way to eliminate the waste from all of their processes. This elimination of waste was not a weekly or monthly process, but a daily process that required total participation from everyone in the organization. We eliminate this waste through the daily *kaizen* and the fundamental principle that propels us to eliminate this waste is *mottainai*!

Lastly, I am deeply grateful to the Japanese people for all they have taught me. At the core, they are very simple people who have deployed a beautiful and effective philosophy about the way they live. At the same time, the simplicity of how they live out this beautiful stewardship allows them to deploy sophisticated systems that enhance the lives of millions of people. It is the simplicity of teaching gratitude, with something as basic as the short prayer they say before every meal (*Itadakimasu*). It is further supported by a *mottainai* mentality.

So come to Japan to see in-depth and in-person this amazing culture. Perhaps you too will be walking down the street and have a *satori* (sudden enlightenment) moment. For me, the epiphany of banishing sloppiness and falling in love with precision began one of the most important journeys of my life. My hope and prayer is that this book might also begin a journey in your life that creates greater fulfillment and respect for the abundance and blessings we have all been given.

The One Thing:
Mottainai...what a pity to waste anything!

 For book resources and videos go to paulakers.net/bs-13

CHAPTER 14
Paul's Conclusion

Hopefully, you have enjoyed this book. It has been such an important book for me to write. As a parting comment, I want to say you don't just learn this and then become perfect and precise in one fell swoop. It is a lifelong journey. There will still be mountains of sloppiness and waste everywhere in everything you do. But what is important is you begin the journey today. When you start being more thoughtful and precise in everything you do, you become a better steward of the resources you have been given. Remember, it is not about perfection. It is about starting the journey to perfection. This is the joy I experience every day, knowing that I am more thoughtful of the gifts that I have been given. Being wasteful benefits no one, but good thinking benefits everyone.

 The One Thing:
Good Thinking...Good Life!

 For book resources and videos go to paulakers.net/bs-14

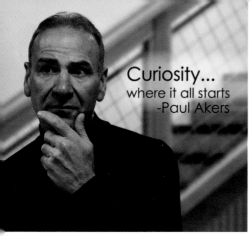

Curiosity...
where it all starts
-Paul Akers

Paul Akers is the founder and president of FastCap, a product development company specializing in woodworking tools and hardware for the professional builder. FastCap was started in Paul's garage in 1997 when he simply "fixed what bugged him" and developed his first product: the Fastcap Cover Cap. From humble beginnings, and no MBA, FastCap has thousands of distributors worldwide in over 40 countries. Paul's intense curiosity on how things could be improved paved the way for him to become a prolific innovator and today he holds many US and International patents. FastCap launches approximately 20-30 innovative products per year and has won business of the year in 1999 and 2010. In June 2011 Paul won Seattle Business Magazine's prestigious Business Executive of the Year award. He wrote his first book, 2 Second Lean, about creating a fun, Lean culture, that, is now available in 15 languages. In 2015, he wrote his 2nd book, *Lean Health*, in 2016, he wrote *Lean Travel* and in 2019, he wrote *Lean Life* and *Banish Sloppiness*. In 2016, Paul's book, *2 Second Lean*, was recognized by the Shingo Institute and won the Research and Professional Publication Award.

Paul learned to embrace adventure and pursue excellence by his father when he earned the rank of Eagle Scout at the young age of 14. At the age of 15, Paul built a guitar in high school woodshop and earned the attention of Bob Taylor, founder of Taylor Guitars. Bob put Paul to work the day he graduated from high school and mentored him, making a lasting impression as Paul watched Bob – a true American innovator – changed the guitar industry right in front of Paul's eyes. In 2017, Paul was honored to document Bob Taylor on his World Forestry Tour where a small team journeyed around the world to increase awareness of sustainable forestry practices.

He graduated from Biola University in 1983 with honors, obtaining a degree in Education.

Paul worked in Pasadena, restoring some of the most prestigious historical homes and became part of an exclusive group of craftsmen that built the home for the editor of Architectural Digest.

Paul taught Industrial Arts at Mark Keppel High School where his innovative thinking led to the development of a program that focused on teaching kids to build furniture, rather than the standard high school projects like key racks and cutting boards.

He catapulted into the business world when his knack for problem solving led to an invention and eventually to his own manufacturing business. Through a series of twists and turns he discovered Lean and the Toyota Production System (TPS) which was instrumental in propelling FastCap as an example of Lean manufacturing and culture, followed by thousands of companies around the world.

In 2010, Paul ran for the US Senate in Washington State on a Lean platform of transforming government by empowering people. After the election, Paul has continued to work with various government agencies teaching Lean thinking and helping them create a Lean culture in government organizations throughout the country. In 2013, Paul was invited to do a TEDx talk on innovation. In 2017, Paul was selected as #3 Individual Thought Leaders & Influencers in The Global State of Operational Excellence, Critical Challenges & Future Trends.

Paul is an avid outdoors man that surfs, runs, swims, bikes, and has summited many 14,000 foot mountains, including Mt. Kilimanjaro, and trekking to Everest Base Camp. Paul is passionate about health and completed 2 ironman (Lake Placid, NY and Vichy, France).

Paul is an instrument rated pilot with over 2,000 hours of flight time, which includes 3 North Atlantic crossings in a single engine plane.

Paul is an energetic speaker whose core passion is helping people discover their full potential and showing others how to implement Lean in their business and personal life. Paul's passion for Lean has taken him around the world to over 104 countries to work and speak with such notable organizations as the Israeli Defense Forces, Mercedes Benz, Amazon, the US Navy, Turner Construction, and many universities. From Kazakhstan to Iceland, Tasmania to Japan, Germany, Israel, Africa and Slovakia, you never know where Paul is ... but for sure he is teaching Lean concepts with passion and excitement. Paul is also passionate about Japan and teaching people the philosophy of this amazing country (Japan Study

Mission). He has trained over 30 teams in Japan at Toyota, Lexus, and their suppliers.

Paul has thousands of followers on his weekly podcast, "The American Innovator" where he teaches about the power of innovation and Lean thinking. He shares his insights and observations as he interviews fascinating people along with documenting his travels and adventures around the world with staggering photography and videography.

Paul has been married to his wife Leanne since 1983 and they have 2 grown children, Andréa and Kolbe, who work with him at FastCap. It is truly a family run business!